COMPUTER CONTROLLED TESTING AND INSTRUMENTATION

COMPUTER CONTROLLED TESTING AND INSTRUMENTATION

An Introduction to the IEC-625: IEEE-488 Bus

Martin Colloms
B.Sc.(Hons.), C.Eng., M.I.E.E.

A HALSTED PRESS BOOK

JOHN WILEY & SONS
New York - - Toronto

Published in the USA and
Canada by Halsted Press, a
Division of John Wiley & Sons, Inc.,
New York.

ISBN 0 470 27406-9
© Martin Colloms, 1983

British Library Cataloguing in Publication Data

Colloms, Martin
    Computer controlled testing and instrumentation.
    1. Microcomputers   2. Minicomputers
    I. Title
    001.64'04   QA76.5

Printed in Great Britain by
The Anchor Press Ltd and bound
by Wm Brendon & Sons Ltd, both of Tiptree, Essex

Preface

The General Purpose Interface Bus or GPIB, developed in the early nineteen seventies, has progressed through several national and international standards to become the widest used and most favoured instrument data and remote control interface system. Over a thousand different types of instruments and computer devices are at present bus compatible and most new designs are manufactured for use with the IEC-625: IEEE- 488 bus. Everyone concerned with control, test systems or instrument purchase should be aware of the GPIB, its power, benefits and its complexities.

Having been involved for a number of years with the GPIB in the course of operating a small electroacoustics laboratory, I became acutely aware of the lack of published information on this subject. Apart from manufacturers own specialised literature, what appears to be most required is a single publication with an overview of both the theory and the wide range of possible applications of the GPIB. The purpose of this book is, therefore, to provide a comprehensive introduction to the bus and to attempt to answer the many questions that arise when implementing a new GPIB test system.

The first two chapters provide a general introduction to the GPIB and its structure leading to a more detailed examination of the bus specification, its cabling, hardware and finally software recommendations. In Chapter 3 controller requirements are fully discussed and many examples of modern units are given. In Chapter 4 a number of applications are described with examples of software. Peripherals associated with the GPIB system and more particularly the controller are surveyed in Chapter 5 and future developments outlined. In the final chapter bus problems and programming hangups are discussed leading to methods of fault detection. Bus analysers and extenders complete the chapter.

Useful additional material includes data codes and interfaces, a listing of GPIB equipment manufacturers, recommended units and symbols, a glossary of terms and a description of interface function capabilities.

Martin Colloms

Contents

1

Introduction to the GPIB

AUTOMATED TESTING

Those involved in electronic testing are well aware of the high cost and complexity of modern test systems. Both their cost and sophistication has increased over the years and the experienced technicians required to operate them are increasingly scarce. A solution which reduces system cost, increases its flexibility and can also remove the need for operator skill is of enormous value, and the IEEE-488 bus promises just that.

Manual testing arrangements involve an array of costly instruments and generators. A skilled operator working to a test manual is required to service numerous time consuming procedures, such as instrument settings, calibrations, plug/cable changeovers and to take readings, which are usually written down in a report. By contrast the advantages of an automated system (ATE) are readily apparent in terms of speed, consistency and operator skill, but at the same time such systems can be very costly. Controlled by a small dedicated computer the operating system is based on programming of a specialised nature to specifically suit the requirements of a test procedure. Implicitly such an installation is inflexible and often requires major redesign and reprogramming by a specialist before additional tasks can be taken on. Nevertheless, where high value product is under test requiring a multiplicity of test steps, or where a large number of items are involved, dedicated automatic test systems are both powerful and cost effective. An area of major growth for these systems has been in the testing of the numerous types of large scale integrated circuits now being produced.

Custom ATE systems generally employ unique internal communication interfaces to send and direct commands and data to the various components of the system, such as digital voltmeters, frequency counters and the like, and these control lines or buses are generally incompatible with those of other manufacturers.

Separate instruments are also available with the elements of a bus interface incorporated. Well-known examples include the BCD (Binary Coded Decimal) used to output data from a variety of digital instruments, from voltmeters to counters, and the RS232, commonly

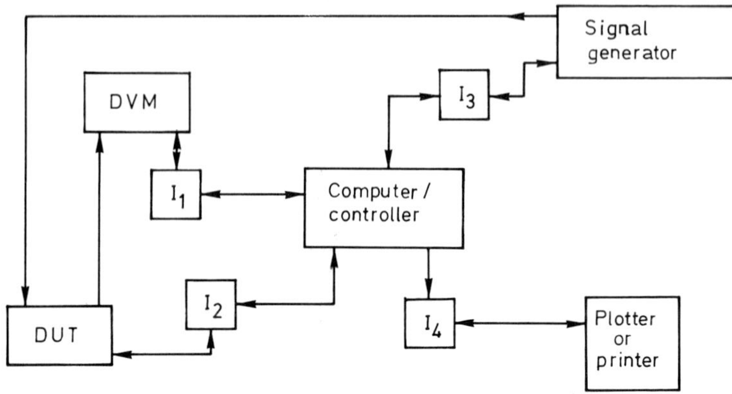

Fig. 1.1(a)   Configuration of early controlled test system. Numerous device orientated interfaces and separate bus cables, each requiring I/O service by the controller with complex programming (I_1–I_4 are separate interfaces)

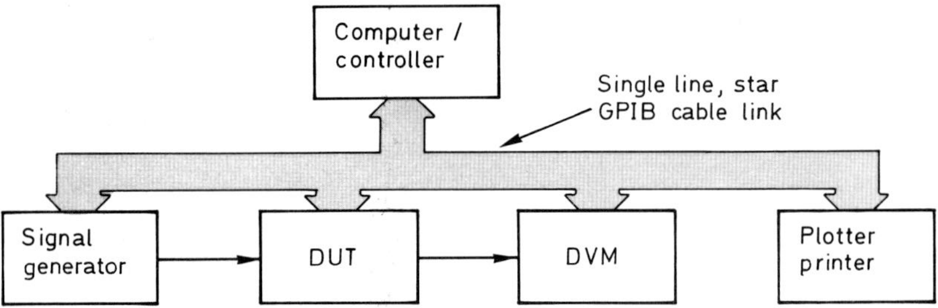

Fig. 1.1(b)   Configuration of GPIB equipment. Only one GPIB I/O port services system with rationalized programming

used for alphanumeric data transfer to peripherals such as a printer. RS232 has also been used in a limited way for driving small 'intelligent' test systems, particularly faster, more specialised installations (Fig. 1.1(a)).

GPIB

It became clear to manufacturers of measuring and test equipment that something more universal and comprehensive was required and a major USA producer took the initiative and developed a logical and more or less comprehensive interface communication design called the HPIB (Hewlett-Packard Interface Bus) (Fig. 1.1(b)). This was largely accepted by other major companies in the early 1970s and

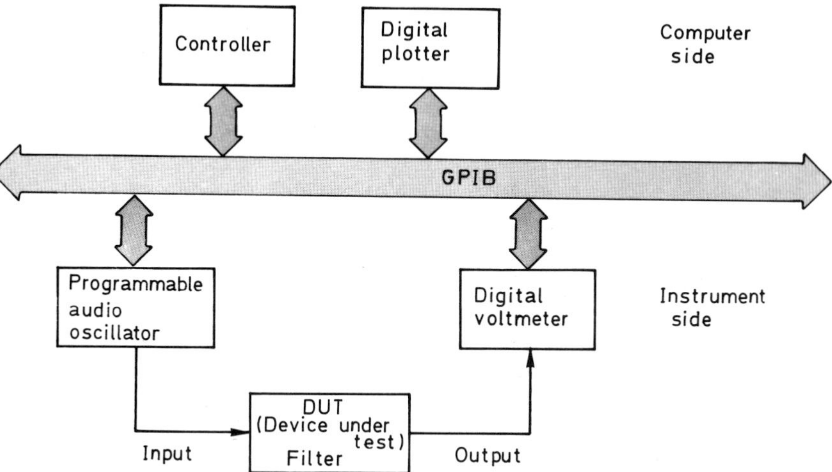

Fig. 1.2   Bus test system for the measurement of amplitude frequency

following study by members of the IEEE professional group
responsible and those of the IEC it was published as the IEEE-488
standard in 1975, updated with minor revisions in 1978, this date
covered by the International Standard IEC 625: 2. HPIB is still used
by its trademark owner; other names include GPIB (General Purpose
Interface Bus) and the ANSI MC1.1-1975. In Europe the IEC
designation is common (this using a different type of connector plug)
and is known as the IEC-TC66/IEC-625 and both this and the GPIB
will be referred to in the book as the GPIB or, in context, the bus.* It is
anticipated that the IEC document will shortly provide for both types
of connector; adaption is relatively simple.

The GPIB is an interface design which allows the simultaneous
interconnection of instruments on a common communication line,
including a computer controller. Facilities exist for the controller to
command instrument operating conditions and direct it to perform
measurements. The resulting data may then be transferred via the
bus direct to a printer or to the controller for visual display, storage or
processing. Groups of instruments may be commanded so as to set up
the complete programming of a measurement of a product under test.

In the arrangement shown in Fig. 1.2, a simple program could
direct the programmable oscillator to output a known voltage level to
the amplifier under test at a number of discrete frequencies. At each
stage the digital voltmeter reads the device output level which is

* BS 6146 is the UK implementation of the IEC-625.

stored by the computer. Gain versus frequency data can then be compared with reference figures in the program for a pass/fail decision, printed numerically or automatically plotted in the form of a conventional amplitude-v-frequency response.

When a test arrangement is no longer required, the units are simply unplugged and may be reorganised with other units and a new program to form a new arrangement, or the separate units may be used individually for normal work.

The basic GPIB standard provides for the interconnection of up to fifteen instruments or devices, this total including the computer/controller. (In Chapter 2, secondary addressing, the extension of this number is described.) It includes methods for the orderly transfer of data, for individually addressing units, and scanning them for their operating conditions. Suggested syntax is given, plus the standard bus management commands, and it operates as a live interactive link between the controller and the units serviced by it.

Units on the GPIB are generally test instruments, but computer peripherals are becoming more common, ranging from mass storage units such as cartridge tape or disc stores, to alphanumeric printers and digital graphics plotters.

TALKER—LISTENER—CONTROLLER

Depending on a unit's capability with regard to the GPIB, it may be classified as a 'talker', e.g. a simple DVM with data output; a 'listener' which can only accept data from the GPIB, such as a printer; or a 'controller' which manages communications on the GPIB, sequencing the correct system operation with appropriate commands. A talker/listener can be a controller, but more specifically it is a sophisticated type of instrument with the ability to accept program and range instructions while addressed as a listener and subsequently to output measured data as a talker (Fig. 1.3).

The numerous and inexpensive computer controllers suited to GPIB duties are generally quite friendly in that they use a simple English-like programming language, a form of BASIC (Beginners Allpurpose Symbolic Instruction Code). They are thus relatively easy to use and reprogram.

GPIB connections are easily made via one locking connector per link and both linear and star arrangements are possible with a good choice of cable lengths.

THE BUS AND COMPATIBLE DEVICES

Among the many attributes of the bus the following should be mentioned:

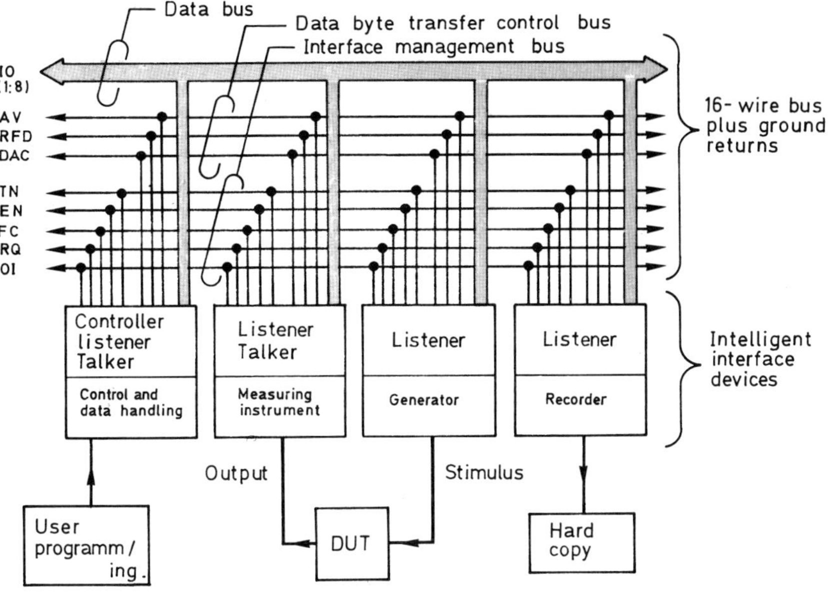

Fig. 1.3   GPIB

(1) The GPIB is potentially quite fast, up to 1M byte transfers per second are possible.

(2) Instruments with differing data rates may generally be interconnected without problems.

(3) It is possible to do without the control device in some instances, the 'high intelligence' of the interface allowing direct communication between some classes of instrument.

Every bus compatible device is adapted to meet the requirements of the interface standard via a built-in GPIB interface, which in itself is usually quite a complex microprocessor based unit. Indeed until recently the high cost of implementing the interface ruled out its use on any but the more costly high performance instruments; however, this is no longer true with the advent of inexpensive dedicated LSI chips designed for GPIB interfacing.

In addition to the required interface functions each instrument possesses its own specialised device functions developed independently of the interface functions. The type of interface also depends on the type of device to be connected to the bus; for example, a simple unit such as a line printer has different needs as compared with a frequency counter. The latter can both receive range command data and output measurements while the printer, in principle, needs only to accept data to print automatically.

Bus devices are classified on a general basis, according to their requirements and facilities, with respect to the bus such as Listeners, which can receive data from other sources. Such devices would include, for example simple printers, display units and signal sources, including programmable power supplies. Talkers are essentially measuring instruments, for example, frequency counters, d.v.m.s, analysers, etc., and can send data to other devices, such as a computer or a printer. The controller controls the flow of data information on the bus and is able to signal which device or devices are to listen and which are to talk. In addition, it can issue special commands required for bus management. Usually the controller function is incorporated in a computer, often a small desktop mini, though it can be included in any instrument if the application warrants it.

The controller acts as a chairman maintaining an orderly and disciplined interchange of information between devices. To do so each device must have a unique address or name and this is provided in the GPIB specification. Following well defined rules the bus is organised so that only one talker at a time may speak on the bus while any number may listen. The data speed or rate is adjusted automatically to suit the comprehension or acquisition speed of the least able listener requiring the information. This is achieved by an effective handshake routine whereby the listeners' signal 'message received' after each information packet has been transmitted on the bus.

The talker/listener/controller distinctions become blurred when the requirements of a more practical controller are accommodated. When programming an instrument remotely, the controller must have a talk mode and additionally a listen facility to acquire information read onto the bus by the responding measuring instrument. By providing separate addresses for the talk and listen sections of an interface it is possible for a given unit to operate simultaneously in talk and listen modes, though this is uncommon. Generally, the unlisten condition is automatically assumed when talking. Many instruments now fit the 'talker/listener' classification; for example, most measuring instruments are programmable and can 'listen' to accept instructions and 'talk' to output data.

While the controller is generally required to make instruments on the bus wake up and pay attention—this done through the address system and the interface control lines—it is possible to construct a simple system omitting the controller. If the devices can be locally or manually set to 'listen only' with only one talker activated, this more or less permanent addressed condition allows the single talker to transmit data to the bus connected listeners.

Only one active controller is permitted at a time but provision is sometimes made for the connection of more than one controller. For example, one controller may be placed in a remote but safe location whilst the other is on site perhaps in hazardous conditions, and control may be passed from one to the other by an appropriate bus command.

BUS OPERATION ANOMALIES

Lest the impression be given that the system is entirely foolproof, the following examples show problems that can arise. One model of an inexpensive computer often used for GPIB duty is in fact non-standard with respect to the bus in certain aspects, notably in the type of connector (PCB edge instead of a proper socket) and also in syntax and available commands. Extra programming is required to deal with the anomalies which in any case are not always soluble. In another situation a full GPIB controller was set up with an instrument, also nominally full GPIB, and hangups were encountered. After investigation it was discovered that the instrument manufacturer's own controllers automatically sent a necessary 'CRLF' character (Carriage Return/Line Feed) following commands. Manual addition of a CRLF to the command statements for the 'independent' controller were required for correct operation. Such details are often omitted from the manufacturer's literature.

STANDARD CODES AND FORMATS

As defined, the GPIB standard falls short of ensuring complete compatibility due to a lack at present of specific code and formats for the data signals communicated. While damage proof electrical compatibility is ensured together with the essentials of a universal command structure, the essence of the communication 'language' is not yet established. In consequence several manufacturers have developed their own formats or interface languages. The format chosen can affect the price of the final product, and such cost pressures have led to system operating differences, with some units possessing a compromised bus capability.

Even the virtually essential SRQ (Service ReQuest) function has been omitted from some units. Their unwitting interconnection can result in system operation failure or a mistranslation of intended commands producing ambiguous bus operation. Skimping at the instrument design stage is largely a thing of the past due to the availability of GPIB, LSI chips which readily allow a full implementation of the bus protocol at relatively little cost and trouble.

At the time of writing the IEEE committee is working on guidelines and recommended practice for data code and format conventions, particularly concerning programmed instructions to instruments, and will be ratified as IEEE 728. It is anticipated that existing mainstream practice will be followed; each message section to comprise a header and a numeric field with an optional separator. IEEE 728 is essentially the US edition of the international document on Code and Formats Guidelines, IEC 625: 2, produced recently.

INSTRUMENT PERFORMANCE ENHANCEMENT

Apart from the important benefits of easily programmed automation an interesting benefit can often result from the addition of a computer, this occurring with a number of the more advanced instruments.

In one case, a digital Fourier spectrum analyser was provided with six main operating modes in its manual or 'local' condition. However, when programmed via the bus from a small computer it became capable of operation in many additional modes, each of considerable engineering value, the total handsomely exceeding the additional cost of the computer!

The presence of a small computer in the development laboratory can be a significant asset in its own right. Design engineers can develop their programming skill and use it for computer aided circuit development.

A very high proportion of new laboratory test instruments are available with a GPIB facility or provided as a low cost option and it clearly makes sense to exploit these facilities. Where competing instruments differ mainly in their provision for bus use, the choice leans heavily in the bus direction.

It is estimated that about 2,000 different types of GPIB oriented instruments and units are available at the time of writing, most of these bus equipped as standard.

ERROR SIGNALLING

A useful feature is the inbuilt intelligence of the GPIB design. If an incorrect command was sent, for example, an out of range setting on a voltmeter, the latter can signal its inability to respond to the command back to the controller, hence alerting the operator.

SIMPLE COMMAND PROGRAM

Consider a simple arrangement of a measuring instrument and a controller with inbuilt printer and display sections (e.g., an HP 85). A program to address the instrument, set a range to take a reading, return the data to the controller and display and print the reading would be as follows:

```
10   INSTRUMENT IS 713     Informs of instrument address
20   DIM A $(10)           Allocates number space for reading
30   OUTPUT 713; 'R3'      Controller commands 'range three'
40   ENTER 713; A$         Instrument returns reading
50   DISP, A$              Controller displays reading
60   PRINT, A$             Controller prints reading
70   END
```

If readings were to be required at specific intervals over a time period, the above program could be modified by the addition of a simple repetitive loop with a 'pause' or time delay statement, resulting in a data logging system.

A few instruments have more advanced programming functions and can output data on the bus directly to a printer without the need for a controller to direct and interface the messages.

2

GPIB structure: hardware, operation, programming and codes

INTRODUCTION

A bus in a general sense is a common group of hardware lines which are used to transmit information between digitally based devices—computers, peripherals, instruments and the like. An interface is designed to organise the orderly and smooth functioning of the data transmitted and handle the fundamental data structure and electrical wiring and system differences between the units connected to a bus.

The GPIB is a bus/interface design which completely covers the four vital aspects concerned, namely hardware, electrical compatibility, data and timing.

PHYSICAL AND ELECTRICAL DETAILS

The GPIB comprises a plug connected cable generally employing a total of 24 wires, seven used for signal ground return, 16 for signals proper and one, usually braided, the main ground return, which links the chassis/frames of the instruments on the bus. Resistance limits maximums for the main return braid and the other signal lines are respectively 0.085 ohm/m and 0.14 ohm/m (Fig. 2.1). An upper capacitance limit of 150 pF/m is specified (applies for any one signal line to all other lines).

While the use of additional signal wiring in the cable is not prohibited, good results have been obtained by forming the six wire handshake and control group into twisted pairs with eight ground signal returns, thus minimising crosstalk. Most interface cables are built this way.

By incorporating the complex interface functions in the equipment to be connected, the interface cable can be entirely passive in nature. The cables parallel all instruments, including the controller, on to the bus and the connectors used are normally stackable allowing easy loom formation without recourse to inverse soldered connections or

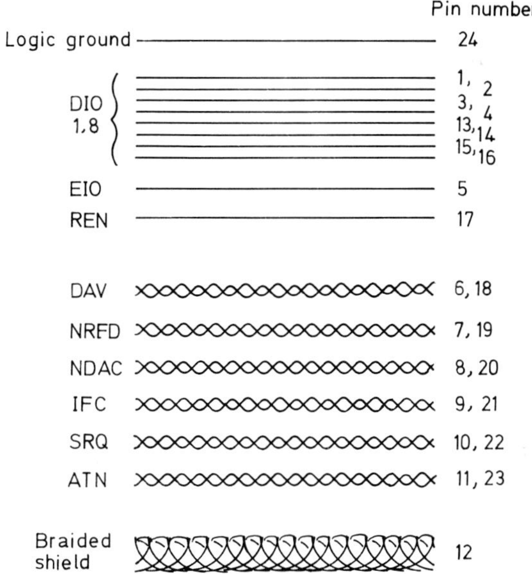

Fig. 2.1   GPIB cable wiring

other complications found on other connection systems (Fig. 2.2(a), (b) and (c)).

The alternative IEC connector is of a 25-pin type allowing an additional ground signal, usually for pairing with the EIO line, but is otherwise fully compatible. Adaptors for connector conversion are available.

Cable radiation and screening

The interconnect cable when carrying data is a potential source of unwanted electrical interference, EMI or EMC, and conversely is susceptible to external interference which may result in false or corrupted data. The standard specification does provide a good measure of protection but where a particularly high standard is required, for example, when a radio transmitter and/or sensitive receiver is involved, further precautions may be necessary. IEC suggestions for improvement include a minimum of 85% braid covering the cable for screening, with up to 90% offering further gains, this enhanced by the addition of metallised film or foil. Also the overall cable grounding is made via the appropriate connection pins

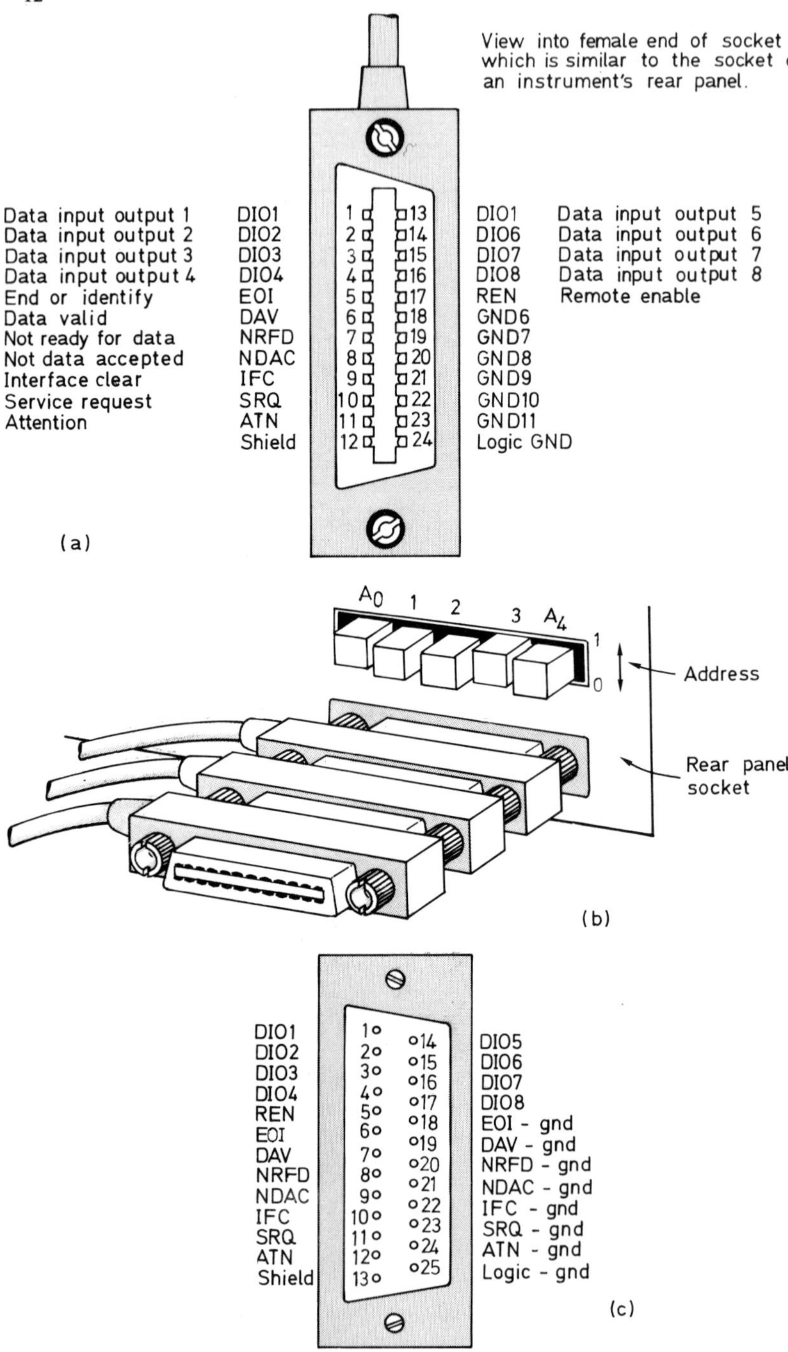

Fig. 2.2(a)   Cable connector (GPIB). (b) Stacking plugs and address switches. (c) IEC connector

and this should be augmented by a good RF ground from the instrument chassis to the metal housing of the connector; the latter recommendation helps screen the connector wiring. Finally, the ground links between the various ground pins (not the logic grounds) and chassis should be as short as possible, preferably less than a few centimetres.

Bidirectionality

In common with most bus systems, the input and output data share the same set of interconnecting wires, and the bus is therefore bidirectional.

By suggesting at the outset the use of open collector, line drivers with pull-up resistor loads at the terminations, the bus provides for parallel connection of many interface junctions.

A maximum inter-unit cable length of 4 m is specified with a total connected length of not more than 20 m. It is possible to add bus extenders which either through buffering or more commonly by data conversion can take the bus to almost unlimited lengths. A bus to serial data converter could, via a modem, be used to remotely control instruments via the telephone network (see Chapter 6). Optic fibre transmission units are also available as extenders for runs of 100 m or more.

Data rates

Quoted data transfer rates of 0.25 M bytes/s are considered the maximum for a normal full 20 m cable bus system used with logic drivers of the open collector type. The use of tri-state Schottky logic drivers can double the rate, theoretically 1 M byte/s is attainable with a maximum cable length of 15 m. This target also necessitates standard logic loads at one metre maximum cable intervals, together with terminal line input capacitances of 50 pF or less. Generally, standard loads are specified at 2 m intervals with an associated input capacitance limit of 100 pF.

The fastest data rates can only be achieved when, in addition to the above considerations, the instruments themselves can operate at these rates, this including the acceptance speed of the controller or listener. In many practical systems data rates of 1 to 10 k byte/s are more typical.

The requirement for active loads at each cable junction necessitates that 50% or more of the units on a given system must be 'powered on'

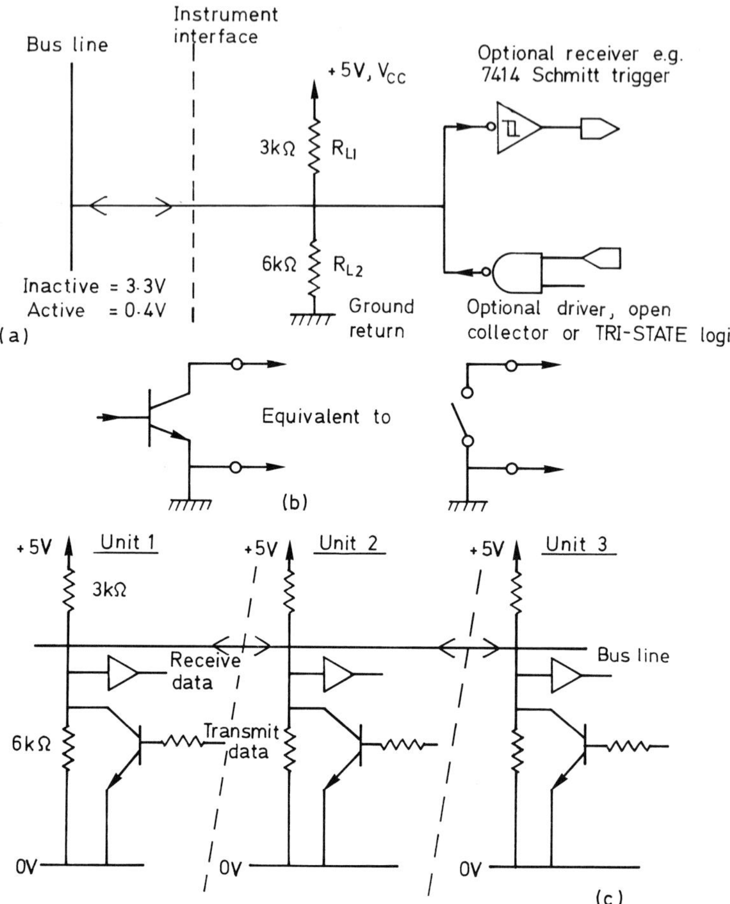

Fig. 2.3   (a) GPIB standard load (approximately 2 kΩ). (b) Open collector driver. (c) GPIB line section

for the GPIB to operate reliably, even if more than 50% of the units connected are not actually involved in bus operations for that test configuration.

Each of the 16 bus signal lines must see a 'standard load' at each junction (Fig. 2.3(a), (b) and (c)). All bus signal lines are TTL compatibly coded so that True or ON is implied when a line is LOW or near ground, but the lines are modified by the addition of a potential divider bridging them to the rails. The latter's equivalent impedance is 2 kΩ, and when the line is open, i.e. released or OFF, the divider(s) lift the line to the divided ratio of the $+5V$ supply, namely $+3.3V$. The divider supplies the line charging current which open collector drivers cannot provide.

INTERFACE FUNCTIONS

Data on the bus as a whole is routed and organised to provide a number of device functions with respect to the bus including Handshake, Talk, Listen, Service Request, etc. The bus interface control, often now in one or two chip form, decodes the bus signals and implements the required functions in the instrument (Fig. 2.4).

The data bus

In general we have used the term bus to refer to the GPIB, but in this instance it concerns the data bus. An 8-line bus is used for data transfer, the information transmitted in the form of a sequence of 8-bit characters, each known as a 'byte'. The ASCII seven-bit code is generally used with the eighth bit employed for parity checking. The ASCII set includes the familiar upper and lower case characters, plus signs, digits, punctuation marks and some 30 control characters, e.g., line feed, making a total of 128 (Table 2.1).

The data bus carries both interface or GPIB messages and device dependent data, such as measurement readings—the state of the ATN control line indicates which is which. If ATN is low or 'on', a bus message is indicated, if high or 'off', then the data is in ASCII form from a device. The data lines are coded DIO (Data In/Out) and are numbered DIO 1–DIO 8. The data form is called bit parallel, byte serial, i.e., each byte appears as parallel bits on the data lines, the complete bytes sent sequentially (Table 2.1).

Message control

Information blocks transmitted over the bus are classed as remote messages, associated either with the interface or the device, with further subdivision into single and multi-line messages. The latter are coded information, such as an address transmitted over the data bus in conjunction with the handshake. As implied, single line messages are dedicated controls sent via the five general interface management lines, such as interface clear (IFC) and service request (SRQ). Device dependent messages include items such as measurement data and instrument control panel status data.

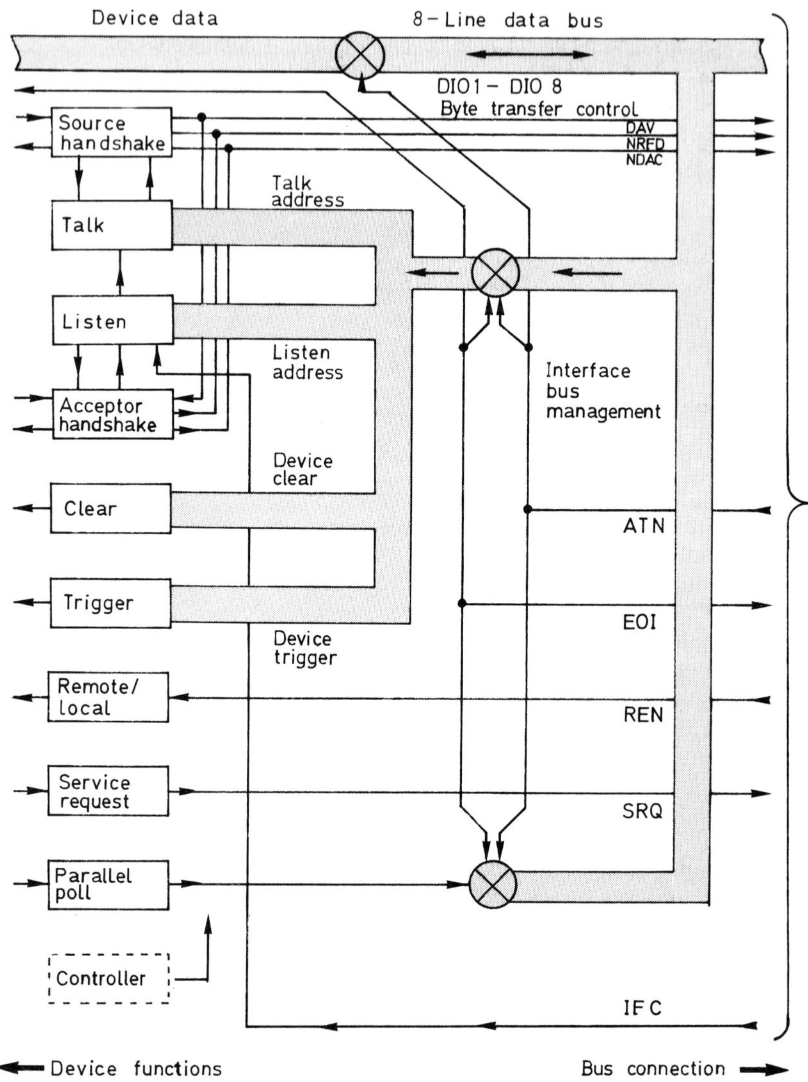

Fig. 2.4   GPIB implementation of device function (courtesy Electronic Design)

Addresses are multiline messages used to determine which devices are to be talkers and which are to be listeners.

Universal Commands direct every compatible instrument on the bus to perform the required interface function and include both single and multiline messages.

Table 2.1. TALK AND LISTEN ADDRESS CODES (AFTER HEWLETT-PACKARD)
(ASCII to 7 bit)

	Listen addresses									Talk addresses									
	Bits								ASCII character	Bits								ASCII character	5-bit decimal code
	b_8	b_7	b_6	b_5	b_4	b_3	b_2	b_1		b_8	b_7	b_6	b_5	b_4	b_3	b_2	b_1		
1	×	0	1	0	0	0	0	0	SP	×	1	0	0	0	0	0	0	@	1	00
2	×	0	1	0	0	0	0	1	!	×	1	0	0	0	0	0	1	A	2	01
3	×	0	1	0	0	0	1	0	"	×	1	0	0	0	0	1	0	B	3	02
4	×	0	1	0	0	0	1	1	≠	×	1	0	0	0	0	1	1	D	4	03
5	×	0	1	0	0	1	0	0	S	×	1	0	0	0	1	0	0	D	5	04
6	×	0	1	0	0	1	0	1	%	×	1	0	0	0	1	0	1	E	6	05
7	×	0	1	0	0	1	1	0	&	×	1	0	0	0	1	1	0	F	7	06
8	×	0	1	0	0	1	1	1	'	×	1	0	0	0	1	1	1	G	8	07
9	×	0	1	0	1	0	0	0	(	×	1	0	0	1	0	0	0	H	9	08
10	×	0	1	0	1	0	0	1	)	×	1	0	0	1	0	0	1	I	10	09
11	×	0	1	0	1	0	1	0	*	×	1	0	0	1	0	1	0	J	11	10
12	×	0	1	0	1	0	1	1	+	×	1	0	0	1	0	1	1	K	12	11
13	×	0	1	0	1	1	0	0	'	×	1	0	0	1	1	0	0	L	13	12
14	×	0	1	0	1	1	0	1	−	×	1	0	0	1	1	0	1	M	14	13
15	×	0	1	0	1	1	1	0	.	×	1	0	0	1	1	1	0	N	15	14
16	×	0	1	0	1	1	1	1	/	×	1	0	0	1	1	1	1	O	16	15
17	×	0	1	1	0	0	0	0	0	×	1	0	1	0	0	0	0	P	17	16
18	×	0	1	1	0	0	0	1	1	×	1	0	1	0	0	0	1	Q	18	17
19	×	0	1	1	0	0	1	0	2	×	1	0	1	0	0	1	0	R	19	18
20	×	0	1	1	0	0	1	1	3	×	1	0	1	0	0	1	1	S	20	19
21	×	0	1	1	0	1	0	0	4	×	1	0	1	0	1	0	0	T	21	20
22	×	0	1	1	0	1	0	1	5	×	1	0	1	0	1	0	1	U	22	21
23	×	0	1	1	0	1	1	0	6	×	1	0	1	0	1	1	0	V	23	22
24	×	0	1	1	0	1	1	1	7	×	1	0	1	0	1	1	1	W	24	23
25	×	0	1	1	1	0	0	0	8	×	1	0	1	1	0	0	0	X	25	24
26	×	0	1	1	1	0	0	1	9	×	1	0	1	1	0	0	1	Y	26	25
27	×	0	1	1	1	0	1	0	:	×	1	0	1	1	0	1	0	Z	27	26
28	×	0	1	1	1	0	1	1	;	×	1	0	1	1	0	1	1	[	28	27
29	×	0	1	1	1	1	0	0	<	×	1	0	1	1	1	0	0	/	29	28
30	×	0	1	1	1	1	0	1	=	×	1	0	1	1	1	0	1	]	30	29
31	×	0	1	1	1	1	1	0	>	×	1	0	1	1	1	1	0	∩	31	30

× = don't care.

Addressed Commands are similar to the universal commands except that they are directed only to the addressed devices.

Handshake operation

A key element of bus operation is the inclusion of a foolproof interlocking of devices sending and receiving data such that correct transfer is achieved despite widely varying intrinsic data handling speeds for the devices. This is the 'handshake' system which can operate asynchronously allowing 'fast' and 'slow' devices to work together on the GPIB, providing for the slowest listener to synchronise the talker to output data at a compatible rate. A slow printer accepting from a fast DVM is such a case. However, when the printer is not being addressed and is thus quiescent on the bus, the data rate will automatically rise to the speed dictated by the next slowest listener addressed.

The 'handshake' works through three signal lines whose states and timing patterns control the data byte transfers. A listener, when signalled or addressed, returns an indication when it is ready and able to accept a data byte. The talker then signals that data is present on the eight-wire data group, so that the listener can then read it into its interface registers.

The three handshake lines are designated NRFD (Not Ready For Data), DAV (DatA Valid) and NDAC (Not Data ACcepted). If high, or 'off', their meaning is respectively '*ready* for data', 'data *not* valid' and 'data *is* accepted' (Fig. 2.5).

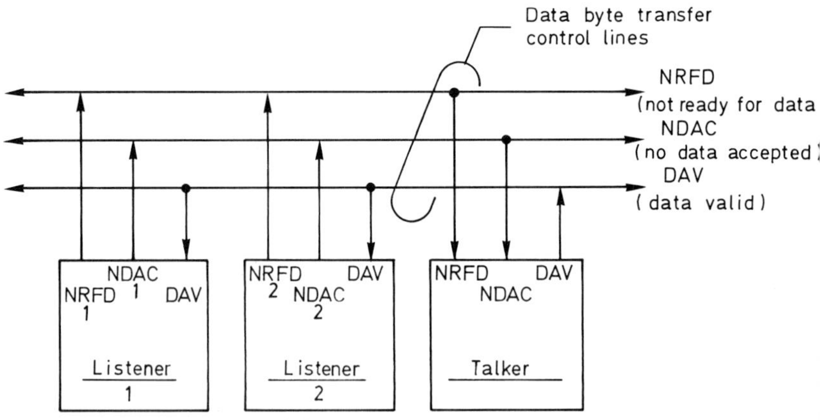

Fig. 2.5   Three-wire handshake

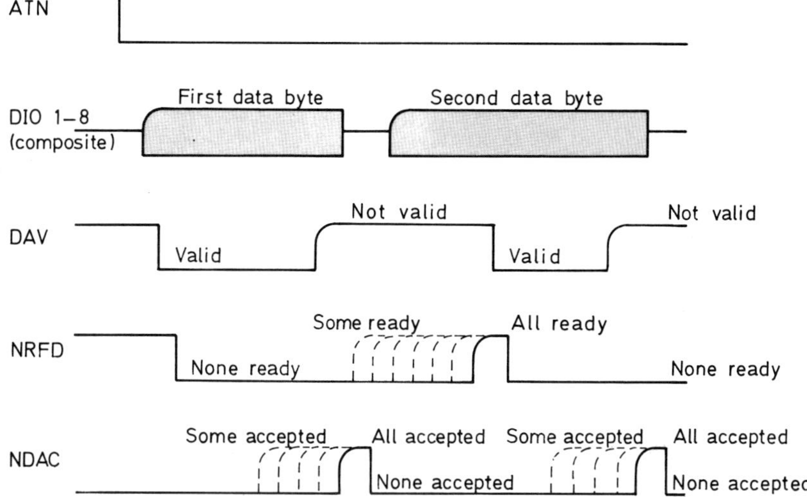

Fig. 2.6   Handshake routine timing sequence

Remembering that a logic high implies that their named conditions are *not* true, the handshake sequence can begin with the controller having released the DAV line high, indicating 'invalid data' as a starting condition. The listeners, previously addressed, then set NDAC lines low to signal 'unaccepted' data. When the controller has checked for invalid conditions such as a failure to sense lows on the NDAC line (NRFD can also be low here), the data byte appears on the data bus and transfer can begin (Figs. 2.6 and 2.7). When ready to accept data the listeners set NRFD high by releasing it, this sensed by the talker and resulting in its reply, a low on DAV signalling data valid. Data transfer now takes place; the controller signals the end of the byte by releasing the DAV line to high, which is sent slightly in advance to help minimise operating delays. Eventually all the listeners signal data accepted when the last of them finally releases the NDAC line to high. Both the NDAC and NRFD lines are wired-OR functions such that they can only be released when all units connected have released.

Once the sequence begins the talker or perhaps controller waits for a short period, typically $2\mu s$, until the DIO line condition is stable (post ringing) and the NRFD line has gone high. This condition met, the talker then pulls DAV low signalling the presence of valid data. In reply the listeners pull NRFD low, blocking a second data byte transfer until the existing byte transfer is completed. Acquiring data at their own rates the listeners, on their individual completion, release

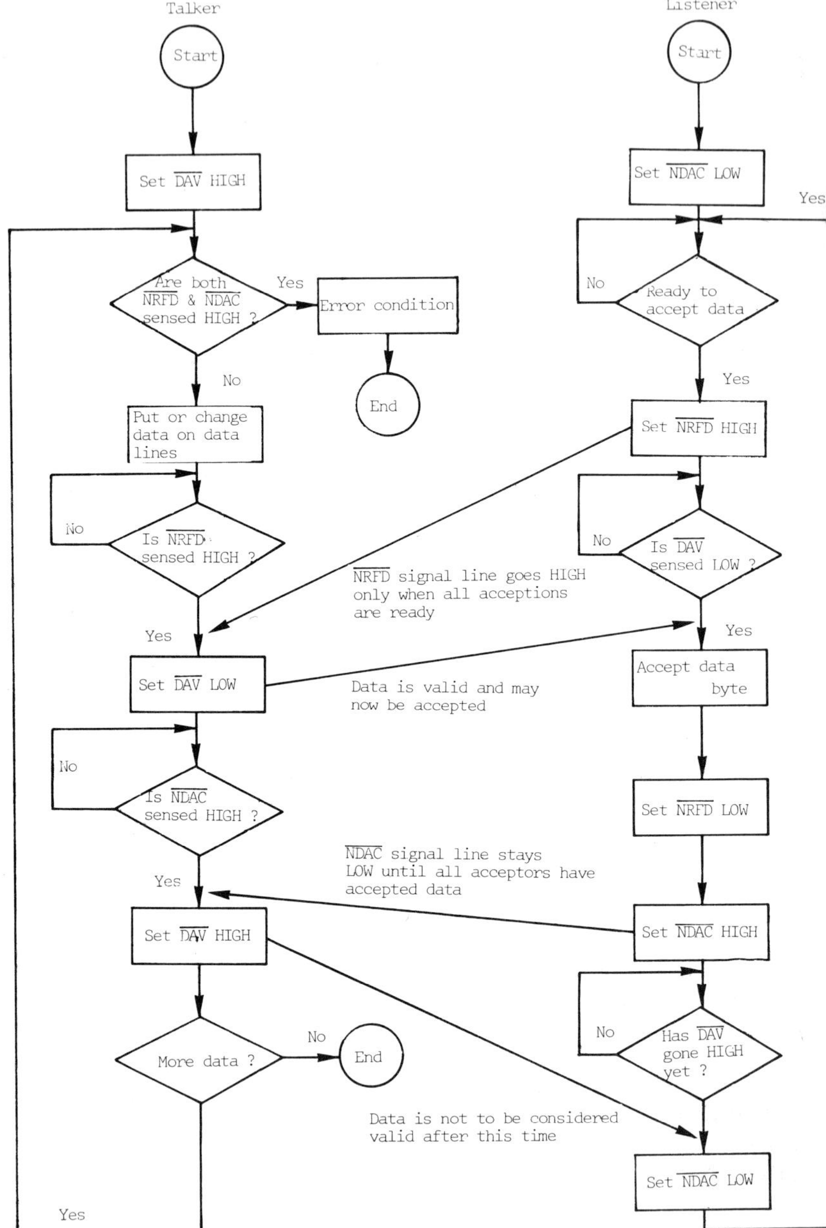

Fig. 2.7   Source and acceptor handshake logic (courtesy Fairchild)

their NDAC lines; the line itself not released until all have released. Once high, the controller reads the 'data accepted' signal and in turn releases the DAV high to indicate completion of the transfer sequence and that data is no longer valid. The listeners then complete the handshake by pulling NDAC low again thus regaining the starting condition ready for the next transfer.

A passive listener if not addressed in a particular communication will set both its NRFD and NDAC outputs high (i.e. open circuited or 'off') and will thus take no part in the handshake and transfer sequence, and will not affect the data transfer rate.

Interface management lines

The remaining five signal lines are allocated to 'interface management' and comprise the 'control bus'. These direct secondary functions, such as the controller function ATN (ATtentioN), specify whether information on the data bus is to be interpreted as an interface control message (MSG IEEE) or as device dependant data. The controller alone drives the ATN line and when 'on' or low directs all devices to release control of their interface lines within 0.2 μs and listen to or read the data bus. This is an interrupt allowing recommencement of the handshake.

The other four management lines are IFC (InterFace Clear), EOI (End Or Identify), SRQ (Service ReQuest), and REN (Remote ENable), the latter also a controller only function which when 'on' directs an instrument to transfer control of its otherwise manually set or 'local' front panel to a 'remote' programmable condition when properly addressed via the GPIB. When the controller sets IFC low all GPIB interfacers are reset to a known quiescent operating state, halting bus talking.

A talker such as a DVM may set the EOI line low to signal the end of a multiple byte data transfer, or if set by a controller it would initiate a polling sequence to scan the status of the devices on the bus. To attract the controller's attention during polling, any device can signal by pulling their SRQ output low indicating a request for service, these requests sequentially scanned by the controller for device identification (see Fig. 2.4).

Polling

The polling sequences allow units to signal the controller and the controller to assess the state of those units.

Serial polling is most common and operates automatically as a part of the bus design when initiated by a device request. Parallel polling also has its advantages and can offer a useful speed gain but requires a small subroutine to be incorporated in the measurement system program, initiated periodically by the controller.

Serial poll allows the SRQ signalling device to give information about the nature of the service request, while in parallel poll the data lines are in use and this is not possible.

It is, however, possible to exploit the best features of both systems. The serial poll sequence is allowed to continue to the SRQ message, at which stage the controller runs a rapid signalling device identification via the parallel poll. Once identified the serial poll mode may be reinstated allowing that device to read back the nature of its service request via the STB message (STatus Byte).

Serial poll

The controller is alerted to a problem or device signal for service by a low or 'on' condition for the SRQ (Service ReQuest) line. Unit(s) may be in an invalid condition such as an over-range, or may simply be indicating that a measurement is complete. The controller response to an SRQ is an interface message on the data bus, the Universal Command SPE (Serial Poll Enable)*, identified as such by an ATN signal from the controller, maintained throughout the poll. After the SPE, the first device on the bus is signalled via its listen address, and it is polled by the controller releasing ATN to off, at which stage the device reads back its Status Byte on the data bus defining its operating condition—be it correct, complete, or in fault or error.

In its simplest form the status byte may just be a low on the DIO-7 line which is a confirmation that the device was responsible for an SRQ. Lows on the remaining DIO lines (the data bus) may signal why the SRQ line was set.

On acceptance of the status byte the controller once again sets ATN low outputting the address of the next device, the sequence finishing when all the devices on the bus have been sequentially polled. After the last instrument has reported, the controller sends the SPD (Serial Poll Disable) universal command.†

If during the poll the operator takes appropriate action after each device is identified, e.g., by loading fresh paper in a printer after it has signalled an exhaustion of its supply, that device's SRQ line output is released. If it was the only unit requesting service the poll would end at that stage.

* The ASCII character sent is 'CAN' or in octal code 030.
† ASCII 'EM', octal 031.

The decision whether to respond to an SRQ is dependant on the controller operating program, and if directed to respond will terminate present bus operation, disengage talker-listener operations via the unaddress command (c.f.) and proceed with the serial poll, addressing units in the order of their program listing.

Parallel poll

The parallel poll is less common in GPIB systems, but is a defined function though lacking the SRQ 'flag' which can be reset as a result of a serial poll. However, under program control a parallel poll of up to eight units can be completed very rapidly, 0.25 ms typically, and this brief scan can be set up for frequent periodic execution.

The controller designates a data line for each device from DIO-1 to DIO-8, accomplished by instruction from the controller, while the addressed device is in the listen mode. The controller sends a PPC (Parallel Poll Configure) addressed command followed by a PPE (Parallel Poll Enable), the latter comprising a 3-bit code identifying one of the 8 data lines, this code stored by the addressed device. To signal the SRQ equivalent the listener pulls its assigned data line low during the parallel poll routine, this carried out when the controller periodically sends an EOI (End Or Identify) together with the ATN line low or on. When either EOI or the ATN signals cease, the controller stops polling. (Some sources cite the IDY command (Identify) (see Appendix 1.)

In practice the number of devices addressed may be extended beyond eight by sharing the DIO line codes with more than one device when so required.

Commands

When the controller activates the ATN line calling for attention, it is in command. All other devices rest in 'listen' mode awaiting controller instructions, of which several groups are defined; address, universal, unaddressed.

Addresses

Both talker and listener address are in individual 7-bit codes, enabling devices to individually talk when uniquely addressed by a controller. If a controller issues a new address while a previously addressed device was still talking, the earlier one is cancelled or 'unaddressed' thereby preventing any confusion in the data output.

Table 2.2. OCTAL CODE CONVERSION (AFTER HEWLETT-PACKARD)

Bits:	b_8	b_7	b_6	b_5	b_4	b_3	b_2	b_1	Octal	code	
	'2'	'1'	'4'	'2'	'1'	'4'	'2'	'1'			
Weights:	(hundreds)		(tens)			(ones)					
	1	0	0	1	1	0	1	0	2	3	2
	1	1	1	1	1	0	0	0	3	7	0
	0	1	0	0	1	0	1	1	1	1	3
	0	0	0	1	0	1	1	1	0	2	7

Note: In Table 2.1 the 'hundreds' group has only one bit since the address code is seven bit ASCII. In octal the single 'hundreds' bit takes the value '0' or '1'.

The 7-bit code is also issued to direct up to 14 devices to listen, with individual direction also provided for (Table 2.1).

Data producers or talkers normally recognise a single byte address, and a specific group of 31, 7-bit ASCII characters are assigned for these.

Data bytes, including addresses, sent on the 8-line (bit) data bus may be shown in octal code form. The conversion or translation is effected by separating the binary bits into groups of three, moving from right to left. Taking each separated group individually each bit is respectively assigned 'weights' of 1, 2, 4, these also allocated from right to left. The sums of the weighted bits in each group then make up the octal numbers in the respective columns (Table 2.2).

Additionally, certain devices can recognise two-byte long addresses and are called extended talkers. The unique talk address of each device can usually be changed, often by altering the setting of a switch array on the instrument's rear panel. Bits numbered 1 to 5 may be set high or low, allowing alteration of the talk/listen addresses.

Units with a listener capability can also exist in extended form, accepting two-byte extended addresses.

Units with both talk and listen addresses have codes assigned pairwise, e.g., the 'listen' character on line five, Table 2.1; the ASCII 'S' is matched by talk character ASCII 'D' and alteration of one automatically rematches the other.

Universal commands

Regardless of address, any device capable of responding to a Universal Command will do so at any time. For example the SPE (Serial Poll Enable) is just such a command (Table 2.3).

Table 2.3. UNIVERSAL COMMANDS

Command	ASCII character	Octal code	Purpose
LLO (Local Lockout)	DC1	021	Disables front panel local-reset button on responding devices.
DCL (Device Clear)	DC4	024	Returns all devices capable of responding to pre-determined states, regardless of whether they are addressed or not.
PPU (Parallel Poll Unconfigure)	NAK	025	Sets all devices on the GPIB with Parallel Poll capability to a predefined condition.
SPE (Serial Poll Enable)	CAN	030	Enables Serial Poll mode on the bus.
SPD (Serial Poll Disable)	EM	031	Disables Serial Poll mode on the bus.

Addressed commands

Though similar to the universal commands, addressed commands are accepted only by those listeners specifically addressed. By issuing a group of appropriate addresses the controller can simultaneously command a selected group of instruments (Table 2.4).

Unaddressed commands

Two commands are available to cancel a previously addressed system condition. One is known as UNL (UNListen) and the other as UNT (UNTalk), and they respectively clear the bus of listeners and talkers. Talkers may additionally be unaddressed or cleared if the controller transmits an unused talk address on the data bus (Table 2.5).

Command mode code

Specified in the Command mode, the code is given in Table 2.5, showing bit levels and their ASCII character equivalents on the DIO 1–7 data bus (Table 2.6).

While the address and command or control codes are specified, there is no specific code for the data inputs or outputs. Devices communicating in the data mode must therefore agree on the meaning of the data code in use, but but hopefully the IEEE will offer

Table 2.4. ADDRESSED COMMANDS

Command	ASCII character	Octal code	Purpose
SDC (Selective Device Clear)	EOT	004	Returns addressed devices, capable of responding to pre-determined states.
GTL (Go to Local)	SOH	001	Returns responding devices to local control.
GET (Group Execute Trigger)	BS	010	Initiates a simultaneous pre-programmed action by responding devices.
PPC (Parallel Poll Configure)	ENQ	005	This command permits the DIO lines to be assigned to instruments on the bus for the purpose of responding to a parallel poll.
TCT (Take Control)	HT	011	This command is given when the active controller on the bus transfers control to another instrument.

Table 2.5. UNADDRESSED COMMANDS

Command	ASCII character	Octal code	Purpose
UNL (UNListen)	—	077	Clears bus of all listeners.
UNT (UNTalk)	—	137	Unaddresses the current talker so that no talker remains on the bus.

recommendations on this subject soon. Programmable instruments are in any case usually provided with an extensive listing of their codes and allowable commands (note, Table 2.7 is an excellent combination of the previous examples.

Other important interface commands

DCL (Device Clear) will clear all instruments on the bus provided with the function to a predetermined state and as such is a universal command. If an address (or addresses) precedes it, SDC (Selective

Table 2.6. GPIB CODE CHART

Key format (per cell): octal (top-left), GPIB code (top-right), ASCII character (center), hex (bottom-left), decimal (bottom-right).

B4 B3 B2 B1	CONTROL (B7B6B5 = 000)	CONTROL (001)	NUMBERS SYMBOLS (010)	NUMBERS SYMBOLS (011)	UPPER CASE (100)	UPPER CASE (101)	LOWER CASE (110)	LOWER CASE (111)
0 0 0 0	NUL (0/0/0)	DLE (20/16/10)	SP (40/32/20)	0 (60/48/30)	@ (100/64/40)	P (120/80/50)	` (140/96/60)	p (160/112/70)
0 0 0 1	SOH (1/1/1)	DC1 GTL (21/17/11)	! (41/33/21)	1 (61/49/31)	A (101/65/41)	Q (121/81/51)	a (141/97/61)	q (161/113/71)
0 0 1 0	STX (2/2/2)	DC2 (22/18/12)	" (42/34/22)	2 (62/50/32)	B (102/66/42)	R (122/82/52)	b (142/98/62)	r (162/114/72)
0 0 1 1	ETX (3/3/3)	DC3 (23/19/13)	# (43/35/23)	3 (63/51/33)	C (103/67/43)	S (123/83/53)	c (143/99/63)	s (163/115/73)
0 1 0 0	EOT SDC (4/4/4)	DC4 DCL (24/20/14)	$ (44/36/24)	4 (64/52/34)	D (104/68/44)	T (124/84/54)	d (144/100/64)	t (164/116/74)
0 1 0 1	ENQ PPC (5/5/5)	NAK PPU (25/21/15)	% (45/37/25)	5 (65/53/35)	E (105/69/45)	U (125/85/55)	e (145/101/65)	u (165/117/75)
0 1 1 0	ACK (6/6/6)	SYN (26/22/16)	& (46/38/26)	6 (66/54/36)	F (106/70/46)	V (126/86/56)	f (146/102/66)	v (166/118/76)
0 1 1 1	BEL (7/7/7)	ETB (27/23/17)	' (47/39/27)	7 (67/55/37)	G (107/71/47)	W (127/87/57)	g (147/103/67)	w (167/119/77)
1 0 0 0	BS GET (10/8/8)	CAN SPE (30/24/18)	((50/40/28)	8 (70/56/38)	H (110/72/48)	X (130/88/58)	h (150/104/68)	x (170/120/78)
1 0 0 1	HT TCT (11/9/9)	EM SPD (31/25/19)	) (51/41/29)	9 (71/57/39)	I (111/73/49)	Y (131/89/59)	i (151/105/69)	y (171/121/79)
1 0 1 0	LF (12/10/1A)	SUB (32/26/1A)	* (52/42/2A)	: (72/58/3A)	J (112/74/4A)	Z (132/90/5A)	j (152/106/6A)	z (172/122/7A)
1 0 1 1	VT (13/11/1B)	ESC (33/27/1B)	+ (53/43/2B)	; (73/59/3B)	K (113/75/4B)	[(133/91/5B)	k (153/107/6B)	{ (173/123/7B)
1 1 0 0	FF (14/12/1C)	FS (34/28/1C)	, (54/44/2C)	< (74/60/3C)	L (114/76/4C)	\ (134/92/5C)	l (154/108/6C)	| (174/124/7C)
1 1 0 1	CR (15/13/1D)	GS (35/29/1D)	- (55/45/2D)	= (75/61/3D)	M (115/77/4D)	] (135/93/5D)	m (155/109/6D)	} (175/125/7D)
1 1 1 0	SO (16/14/1E)	RS (36/30/1E)	. (56/46/2E)	> (76/62/3E)	N (116/78/4E)	∧ (136/94/5E)	n (156/110/6E)	~ (176/126/7E)
1 1 1 1	SI (17/15/1F)	US (37/31/1F)	/ (57/47/2F)	? UNL (77/63/3F)	O (117/79/4F)	_ UNT (137/95/5F)	o (157/111/6F)	RUBOUT (DEL) (177/127/7F)
	ADDRESSED COMMANDS	UNIVERSAL COMMANDS	LISTEN ADDRESSES		TALK ADDRESSES		SECONDARY ADDRESSES OR COMMANDS	

KEY

octal	25	PPU (GPIB code)
	NAK (ASCII character)	
hex	15	21 (decimal)

Get familiar with ASCII and IEEE-488 codes with the help of this handy table. (Copyright © 1979, Tektronix Inc. All rights reserved. Reproduced by permission.)

Table 2.7. CODE ASSIGNMENTS FOR "COMMAND MODE" OF OPERATION (COURTESY HEWLETT-PACKARD)

(Sent and received with ATN true)

Bits: b7 b6 b5 select the column (b7b6b5): col 0 = 000, col 1 = 001, col 2 = 010, col 3 = 011, col 4 = 100, col 5 = 101, col 6 = 110, col 7 = 111. (2) b4 b3 b2 b1 select the row. MSG = interface message (1).

b4	b3	b2	b1	ROW	0	MSG	1	MSG	2	MSG	3	MSG	4	MSG	5	MSG	6	MSG	7	MSG
0	0	0	0	0	NUL		DLE		SP	MLA ASSIGNED TO DEVICE	0	MLA ASSIGNED TO DEVICE	@	MTA ASSIGNED TO DEVICE	P	MTA ASSIGNED TO DEVICE		MEANING DEFINED BY PCG CODE	p	MEANING DEFINED BY PCG CODE
0	0	0	1	1	SOH	GTL	DC1	LLO	!		1		A		Q		a		q	
0	0	1	0	2	STX		DC2		"		2		B		R		b		r	
0	0	1	1	3	ETX		DC3		#		3		C		S		c		s	
0	1	0	0	4	EOT	SDC	DC4	DCL	$		4		D		T		d		t	
0	1	0	1	5	ENQ	PPC (3)	NAK	PPU	%		5		E		U		e		u	
0	1	1	0	6	ACK		SYN		&		6		F		V		f		v	
0	1	1	1	7	BEL		ETB		'		7		G		W		g		w	
1	0	0	0	8	BS	GET	CAN	SPE	(		8		H		X		h		x	
1	0	0	1	9	HT	TCT	EM	SPD	)		9		I		Y		i		y	
1	0	1	0	10	LF		SUB		•		:		J		Z		j		z	
1	0	1	1	11	VT		ESC		+		;		K		[		k		{	
1	1	0	0	12	FF		FS		,		<		L		\		l		¦	
1	1	0	1	13	CR		GS		–		=		M		]		m		}	
1	1	1	0	14	SO		RS		.		>		N		^		n		~	
1	1	1	1	15	SI		US		/		?	UNL	O		_	UNT	oo		DEL	

Column groups:

- ADDRESSED COMMAND GROUP (ACG) — columns 0 MSG
- UNIVERSAL COMMAND GROUP (UCG) — columns 1 MSG
- LISTEN ADDRESS GROUP (LAG) — columns 2–3 (4)
- TALK ADDRESS GROUP (TAG) — columns 4–5
- PRIMARY COMMAND GROUP (PCG) — columns 2–5
- SECONDARY COMMAND GROUP (SCG) — columns 6–7

NOTES:

(1) MSG = INTERFACE MESSAGE

(2) b_1 = DIO1 ... b_7 = DIO7

(3) REQUIRES SECONDARY COMMAND

(4) DENSE SUBSET (COLUMN 2 THROUGH 5). ALL CHARACTERS USED IN BOTH COMMAND & DATA MODES.

Device Clear) will clear only those devices addressed, with the following command sequence:

```
UNL                    (Unlisten, i.e. to any other talker)
LAD (Device A)         (Listen Address for unit A)
SDC                    (Selective Device Clear)
```

GET (Group Execute Trigger) is a means of initiating measurement via bus control by manual keyboard operation of the computer or by programme sequence. Several instruments may thus be started up simultaneously, e.g.

```
UNL
LAD (Device B)
LAD (Device D)
GET
```

When the GPIB was first designed the possibility existed for completely automated reomote controlled instruments without any user front panel controls and indeed some designs of this type do exist, such as the Radiometer RE256 audio analyser. However, most bus instruments have control panels. To avoid confusion between remote and front panel (or local control) programming some protocol is required. The REN (Remote ENable) line is used to control this latter function and when asserted 'true' together with the instrument addressed, disengages some or all of the front panel. Physical disconnection of the bus allows the instrument REN line to go false or high, automatically returning the instrument to local control. This condition may also be attained by the bus command GTL (Go To Local) and is often also provided by a 'local' push button on the instrument panel.

LLO (Local LOckout) is a command override, useful where an instrument generates a local message RTL (Return To Local) in local mode and fails to respond to REN. LLO will neutralise RTL with the addressed command REN following, providing remote control.

CODES AND FORMATS

Working from the IEC 625-2 document (also now IEEE 728), codes and formats for device dependent messages are outlined. The aim is to provide a good measure of programme or software independence from specific instruments and their unique programming formats and to try and make the programming more universal in readability and application; a system useable with a variety of related instruments from different sources. Inevitably this imposes some restriction on instrument design if it is to conform to the format and code specification, thus tending to narrow the freedom of the designer to develop new control and programming enhancements. It could be argued that a situation without standards might be more favourable to the designer but this would be very unsatisfactory for the user. The user does not wish to be involved in programming idiosyncrasies; he wants straightforward, consistent, easy to program systems which may be readily amended and updated as circumstances require, irrespective of the origins of the system components.

Some flexibility is incorporated in IEC 625-2 in that several alternative related representations are allowed and in this sense it is more of a recommended code of practice than a defined standard. As such the intending purchaser of an instrument or bus device must additionally satisfy himself on the degree of conformance offered by that instrument.

The word 'code' refers to pattern of bits in a device dependent data byte (DAB message) and is generally ISO (or ASCII) seven-bit, as given in the GPIB hardware standard. 'Format' refers to the organisation of data bytes in commonly used device-dependent messages.

Examining the role of the various messages, a simple link of two devices over the bus illustrates their demarcation (Fig. 2.8) and the specification by which they are covered, and whether device or interface dependent. The message groups may be further broken

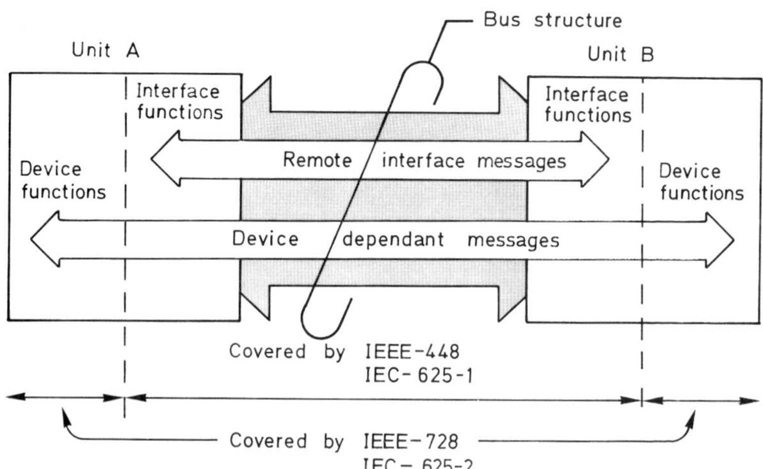

Fig. 2.8   Interface functions and messages (after IEC-625/2)

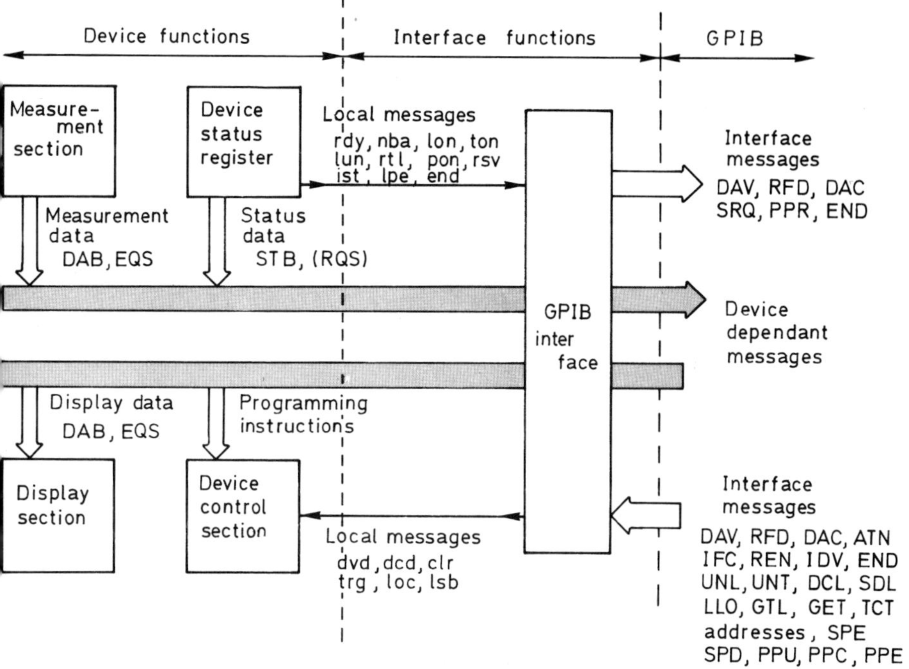

Fig. 2.9   General talker/listener message structure (after Grimberg)

down at the device stage to show their destinations and the internal
structure of a typical talker/listener instrument (Fig. 2.9).

Message structure

For full information it is advisable to consult the Codes and Formats
document since only an outline can be covered in this chapter. A basic
message for measurement or program use is composed of several
elements or fields such as a **HEADER** (generally an alphabetic
character or characters), **DATA** (generally numeric) and a
SEPARATOR, delimiter or end (usually a symbolic character), e.g.
the following fields:

DAB_1 DAB_2 DAB_3 DAB_4
HEADER (HR)   SEPARATOR (SR)   DATA (DR)   SEPARATOR (SR)
                                     Program Instruction or   Message Unit
                                     Measurement Result   Separator

Status byte messages are handled differently and do not utilise the same data fields. STB messages are coded on a single byte using defined subfields.

Header

Taking the header first, it can be used to describe the units present in the following data field or may alternatively select a specific function. Three choices are allowed: alpha, formatted, and a character. With the first, the upper case alphabet is preferred, so a frequency header would be HZ. Where fixed multiple character length headers are helpful in instrument programming the header length may be formatted with embedded or trailing spaces. In the final 'character' header the first 'alpha' may be followed by a number of allowed ASCII/ISO characters and/or a number, e.g. R2, a Range Two program instruction.

While constructions other than alphabetic are allowed the latter does have the advantage of readability which is extremely valuable when writing and reading programs.

Data

The body or data section will include the sign or polarity, the numeric value and finally the exponent notation. Polarity is designated by $+$ and $-$ symbols, but if positive the polarity character is often omitted.

The numeric value is in decimal number form with a decimal point as appropriate. The exponent is a fixed length field consisting of the letter E for a base ten exponent, a $+$ or $-$ character for exponent sign and a numeric value for the exponent, preferably in two-digit form, e.g. $+25.32$ mV could be represented by VOLTS $+25.32E-03/$ separator.

Other numeric representations are allowed and data may also be transferred in other forms, for example, in octal or hexadecimal codes, though with greater instrument intelligence these less friendly forms are becoming less common.

The exponent should be, preferably, in multiples of 3 or one thousandth divisions, thus conforming with the commonly used convention in science and engineering. An overriding preference for message forms which are familiar runs throughout the code and format recommendations and instrument designers should try and follow these as closely as possible. The key aspect is self documentation; the lines of program constituting the bus control messages should ideally need little if any additional explanation or decoding.

Separator/delimiter

Three types of separator are in use depending on the context. To help message processing each message should end with an indicator, though this is not essential. The lowest ranked separator (SR1) has two characters, the comma (,) and the stronger semicolon (;), with the comma preferred.

The next level separator (SR2) is distinctly above SR1 and the traditional character is the ASCII CRLF (Carriage Return Line Feed) derived from early computer printers. The preferred designation is NL (New Line) whose ASCII/ISO character is identical to LF. To aid compatibility it is useful for the time being for instruments to be flexible in their handling of this separator.

SR3 is the highest order delimiter recommended and is usually used when a program or measurement message sequence has been completed, with the implied meaning END, and is sent on the EOI (End Or Identify) line of the bus. As such, when sent, a talker will not output further data bytes unless commanded to do so, manually or by program.

String, block, record

Which delimiter is used also depends on the message unit and structure. A *string* is a sequence of characters or bytes constituting a related data set representing the smallest message unit. A *block* is defined as a sequence of related data strings from one upwards, a single string is also considered a block if it stands alone, unrelated to other strings. A *record* is a sequence of one or more blocks and constitutes the complete device related message. The string, block, record hierarchy corresponds to the SR1, SR2 and SR3 separator rank, e.g. as shown in the following measurement results:

$+22.15 - E3, \ -18.27 - E3,$ END

or

VOLTS $+22.15 - E3, \ -18.27 - E3$ NL VOLTS $20.17 + E3$ END

      (SR1)   (SR2)   (SR3)

Message formats

These fall into four categories; measurement, which we have partially covered in the previous section on message structure, display, status and program instructions.

Display formats are not specifically defined but it is suggested that

Table 2.8. STB FORMAT: STATUS BYTE

Data Lines	8	RQS	6	5	4	3	2	1
TRUE, 1	X or E	Service requested	Abnormal alarm	Busy	X	X	X	X
FALSE, 0	X or not E	Service not requested	Conditions normal	Ready	X	X	X	X

E—Possible extension to device status bits 1–4.
X—Device dependent status data—codes dependent on instrument.
B_6—True if data sent or received is corrupt or erroneous or data is out of limit.
B_5—True if the device is still processing data or responding to instructions.

the measurement and program messages can be used, their particular relevance relating to the character and string data type. Obviously where display messages are concerned the most readable message presentations are the most valuable. Program instructions follow the general message form, though two groups are present, data and commands. When data is sent the separator at the end of the record may function as an execute command for the instruction data sent. The command does not include data and may comprise a single character or examples such as RESET or STOP.

With the program messages instruments may be instructed to alter their operating state in several areas, for example a signal generator may be shifted in frequency and output level and the output switched on. The general form is similar to the measurement message and complex message syntax guidelines are given in the standards (IEC 625-2).

By using special characters in the header and character data field it is thus possible to match program code with similar characters located on the respective front panel control labelling. Such system design helps greatly in software production with hands-on trial of instructions written to some degree directly from the relevant instrument front panel. With such high level program messages, the recommended parsing and syntax construction of the message needs to be carefully followed.

If a hangup occurs, a unit may have been misprogrammed to an unspecified blank range or a measurement may have over ranged; an SRQ service request goes on the bus signalling the controller. The instrument status byte is then available on the DIO_{1-8} data lines with DIO_7 or STB (called RQS) set true indicating that service has been requested.

3

Computer controllers for GPIB; performance, applications and facilities

GENERAL CONTROLLER REQUIREMENTS

A computer-controller has a number of facilities and responsibilities and the type chosen will depend on the functions required. In bus terms therefore the controller is the dominant device on the bus managing the flow of information and issuing commands, etc.

Basically, the controller comprises a black box unit working on-line, managing processes of wide application according to an operating program. The program may have been developed elsewhere and made available to the controller on a transferable memory component such as an EPROM (Erasable Programmable ROM—memory 'chip') or on magnetic storage tape, cartridge or disc.

Clearly operator interaction is neither wanted nor called for with such a simple controller, as its operation is essentially automatic. Where limited supervision and interaction is required, the controller may have available a limited number of labelled special function keys, these traditionally grouped on a conventional typewriter type keyboard but more recently they have also been provided as touch sensitive overlays on a CRT screen. The CRT monitor is a valuable feature for these interactive arrangements in allowing display of instructions and prompts; in the case of the touch overlay they also provide the specific labels for the 'key pads'. To prevent false instructions or even lock-up of an operating program due to inadvertent depression of the wrong key, the more advanced controllers feature electronic masking, whereby areas of the keyboard field not required can be blanked. The latter can also be achieved by using a custom fabricated mask to physically enclose the keys to be masked.

Conversely, in its most complex form, the controller is similar to a full function mini-computer. Many such designs are in fact dual purpose and can carry out advanced calculations and processing duties in addition to the GPIB control. Good programmability allows the designer of the test system to develop the operating programme on the controller and he can be sure that the system works correctly. Controllers are often designed to incorporate advanced in/out sections, their interface programming often contained in ROM units and providing well organised control of major instructions transmitted on the GPIB. These facilities can save very significant expenditure on bus system programming. In the computer field the cost of the software or programming and its development usually exceeds by a large margin the cost of the computer installation itself and, while bus managed systems often include a great deal of costly additional instrumentation, this software versus hardware relationship can still hold true. Wherever possible advantage should be taken of off-the-shelf software, but in the specialist industrial field, few of these packages exist or are applicable. When a company has to produce its own programs, the cost of a more advanced computer controller, which at first sight may seem unnecessarily expensive, will be repaid very quickly if the unit is easier to program or works more readily with the other equipment to be controlled on the bus.

Unavoidably, this can lead to a majority or all of the units making up a system being sourced from one manufacturer. While this might appear to restrict the choice of equipment to those few companies which make a comprehensive range of both instruments and controllers, in most cases, the essential versatility of the bus will allow such limitations to be overcome.

In the early years few controllers were available to drive instruments on the GPIB, but with the introduction of inexpensive bus interface integrated circuits from several major manufacturers and the evolution and improved availability of small 'personal' computers, many bus controllers are now marketed. These range from the simplest dedicated type costing around £700, to relatively high powered computers in the £20,000 range which also offer GPIB facilities. The availability of add-on adaptors to convert virtually any computer with the ubiquitous RS232 series interface to GPIB compatibility further extends the range of units.

There are, nevertheless, distinct advantages in buying a controller whose internal operating system has been designed with bus operation in mind since programming, which is a time consuming activity, is made far easier. General purpose adapted computers are likely to need more experienced programmers to deal with the special syntax and command sequences on the bus which are more or less self evident and automatic with a dedicated bus design.

In specialised applications it may be worth designing a unique controller using the latest integrated circuits available with these facilities such as the Intel 8291, 8292 used with the Intel 8085 8-bit microprocessor.

Programming

Software generation is often performed on the computer controller and the quality of its program language, particularly with respect to the bus and its special requirements, can be a major factor in software cost.

From the test engineer's viewpoint, programming in machine code is unnecessarily difficult and the resulting program is generally unreadable by anyone else in the company. It is well worth examining the program generation side of a controller carefully and making a realistic estimate of software versus hardware costs. For new software the cost is estimated to be between 2 and 10 times the cost of the computer hardware, though the ratio is improved with the programming enhancements provided on the more costly machines. As one experienced engineer put it, 'Estimate the maximum time that you think the software generation requires and then double it!'.

Professional computer programmers often fail to understand why test engineers almost universally use BASIC for GPIB programming. The reason is that test development engineers are not usually programmers and, therefore, they benefit from a language which is easy to learn. The major advantage of using BASIC is that in contrast to many other compiled languages it is an interpretive interactive medium. During the design of a test routine it is vital to be able to try out and sequence programme instructions line by line, and BASIC allows this step by step process, thus greatly aiding the analysis of GPIB problems. Bus commands entered on the keyboard may be sent directly and immediately to an instrument to verify the correct response to a trial instruction.

Areas where the program language enhancement can be very helpful include flexible handling of data formats. An ability to access commonly used subroutines by name is also helpful. Where various block codes are used for data, error trapping routines aid reliability. At the computer level, operator conveniences such as a good display, fast editing facilities and the like are also important.

Controller speed and program comparisons

Some interesting comparisons* of the performance of early controllers and more advanced models, the former represented to some

* Attributed to G. Nelson, Hewlett Packard Inc., at Testmex, London, 1981.

degree by the present-day low cost or adapted types and the latter by more recent and advanced dedicated bus machines, have been made. An early model represented by the HP9830, and first released in 1972, employed rather cryptic ASCII character codes in a 21-line example program to execute a simple bus operation and computation. The associated test instrument imposes a minimum execution time of 50 ms for the routine and the 9830 takes 1,260 ms for its overall execution. The widely used and much faster HP9825 16-bit controller appeared five years later and employed a less cryptic reduced version of the BASIC language called HPL, whose condensed mnemonics gave more user information on its single line LED display. Also, execution time for the routine was much faster at 115 ms.

The latest 1982 version of the controller, the HP9826, runs in a full text, highly enhanced BASIC with much improved user readability. A dramatic speed increase is not evident, the execution time is now 84 ms, close to the instrument limit, but its capabilities in other directions are expected to provide greater improvement in appropriate situations. The Basic language on board is very large at some 300K bytes and contains a number of Fortran and Pascal like enhancements.

When the utilisation of a desktop computer controller are assessed its duties fall into three roughly equal parts, i.e. one third I/O (in/out) intensive, one third program and one third computation. Thus, excess power alone in any one department may not improve the overall system performance significantly.

CONTROLLER ATTRIBUTES

Three main attributes are required from an instrument controller in the following order of priority: reliability, ease of software development, and execution speed.

Reliability is paramount since the investment in an instrument is not just its capital cost but rather its life-cycle cost, including repair and maintenance, which can be very high relative to ordinary laboratory instruments. Further, the test installation under control has an overall cost including software whose return is based on utilisation. The lost production due to failure of a test station in the absence of a replacement controller can quickly exceed the cost of the controller itself.

Digressing a little, reliability is generally proportional to the semiconductor chip count, be they individual transistors or complete LSI circuits. In 1972 an 8-bit central processor unit required 82 integrated circuits with 4000 transistors. By 1981 it was possible to

Table 3.1. ANNUAL COST PER CENT PER THOUSAND POUNDS OF CONTROLLER PRICE

1970	*1975*	*1980*	*1986 (target)*
40%	12%	4%	2%

put 70,000 transistors on one integrated chip. This aspect of computer controller design alone has provided a huge increase in reliability and further steps such as production testing over a wide temperature cycle of 0° to 65°C, thirty or more times in some cases, have also provided gains. HP put the failure rate for their particular controllers on the following basis; the cost annually of failure is put as a proportion of the instrument cost (Table 3.1).

With an average controller costing £2,000–£5,000, it would fail once or twice per year in 1973. The 1980 generation of good-quality machines might be expected to fail once in five to ten years.

When considering a computer the whole system must be taken into account and not just the mainframe itself. Considerations of reliability must also encompass the peripherals—particularly the accessory interfaces needed and the memory store—whether disc or hard electronic. In addition one must consider the temporary power failure problem where the running program may crash and corrupt data on the disc or information held in internal memories may be lost. In this case a machine with a 'graceful' power down capable of protecting and temporarily storing valuable data in the event of power failure could be a great advantage.

Given the high cost of program or software development, which often amounts to the biggest single expense, controllers which ease program development, aid reliable bug-free programs, and which may be easily read and adapted to a new instrument by a different test engineer, are well worth their extra capital cost. In recognition of this fact controllers are emerging with friendlier languages. Ideally programme development should be semi-automatic, carried out on advanced powerful central machines, with the human instructions in more or less plain English.

However, some manufacturers have diverged from the nominally standard **BASIC** generally used for controllers. Racal's controller has been designed around a high level language called **SABRE** whose keywords are derived from another high level language, ATLAS. An example of **SABRE** is shown with its **BASIC** equivalent:

```
SETUP AF GENERATOR, FREQUENCY 3400 HZ   (SABRE)

OUTPUT 703, 'FR3400HZ'                   (BASIC)
```

A halfway stage is offered by some of the newer controllers where a library of subroutines and instrument addresses may be held and these accessed by simple names, as and when required, in the main program.

Some manufacturers have made major efforts to integrate controller and instruments on the bus in order to guarantee a high level of program accuracy and development speed. The Tektronix TM5000 series is a prime example where the controller may even be integrated physically with the instruments in a compact modular rack.

The final factor is execution speed, allied with processing power, this often mistakenly understood as the prime performance factor. Clearly in a given application where a particular test installation is performing a test cycle in, say, 20 minutes and substitution of a more powerful controller provides a 5 minute saving, the productivity is enhanced by 25%. More important than high speed or large memory capacity, is the internal hierarchy of the controller and how quickly it can service its I/O ports. Cases have been known of powerful minicomputers provided with control I/O facilities, including GPIB, where the I/O handling is unacceptably slow, representing a major loss in speed for the system. Generally the more interfaces in use the slower the system runs and multiple interface facilities on controllers should be viewed with this in mind. The quality of GPIB port handling is also important and again some of the large general purpose computers as well as certain add-on adaptors to GPIB are clumsy or incomplete in their design.

Features such as DMA (direct memory access) are important, for example in allowing large data block transfer to a mass storage or memory while servicing bus commands. Finally, it must be conceded that if a large high level language is an important factor then a powerful controller with a large memory is required to handle that language and it is in this context that the high speed of the more advanced controller falls into place.

LOW COST CONTROLLERS

Largely due to its low cost, the Pet computer from Commodore has proved popular for users who are setting up or experimenting with bus systems. It does have an inbuilt interface, nominally to the GPIB standard, but its departures from that standard include a special printed circuit card 'edge' rather than a proper socket, and furthermore the fact that its implementation of the standard is incomplete rules out certain commands and significantly complicates the programming of the remainder. Initially the Pet was specifically orientated towards the home and educational markets. It has, however, evolved with the introduction of more advanced versions incorporating expanded memory from 8K to 32K, improved mass storage, as compared with the earlier slow consumer type audio cassette tape unit plus a professional quality keyboard. Many units can now in fact be seen in industrial applications, and more commonly in business systems.

Examination of an example program required for the PET to handle a simple measurement with a BCD output digital voltmeter (used in conjunction with a bus adaptor) shows a rather inelegant result despite the Pet's use of BASIC, a simple programming language (Fig. 3.1).

Bus dedicated controllers can be programmed with remarkable ease to take measurements from a compatible instrument. For example, in the case of a sophisticated spectrum analyser the HP8566A and an HP9835 controller:

```
10   OUTPUT; 718; 'CF OA'        Controller commands analyser '718'
                                 to activate centre frequency, prepare
                                 to output value present
20   ENTER 718; F                (Value transfers to controller)
30   PRINT 'CENTER
     FREQUENCY ='; 'F; Hz'       (! Print statement for label and unit)
40   END
```

When activated or 'RUN' the computer prints 'CENTER FREQUENCY = 12375 Hz'.

Complications arising with the Pet stem from the fact that the REN line is permanently wired in the 'true' condition, that programme control is not available on the IFC line, that the EOT line moves when the bus is not actually in use, and also the acceptor handshake which controls transmission flow is non-standard. The incorrect timing in talk mode releases ATN before taking control of the NRFD and NDAC lines and only 64 ms is allowed for a reply, too short an interval for many high resolution measuring instruments which may require up to 200 ms.

Some manufacturers have designed ingenious subroutines for their instrument application programming to overcome Pet limitations. In their advanced bus interfaced transient recorder, Datalab use a series of fast machine code routines, accessed within an operating program for the Pet, though with the following limitations. The Pet must be the only controller on the bus, acting as a listener without a specific listen address, and as a talker without a specific talk address. Finally, the normal drive, speed and noise immunity of the general bus specification will not be met.

```
10 PRINT"3    DM141 TEST PROGRAMME" : PRINT
20 M$="2"
30 GOSUB505
32 REM- USING OMNIBUS IN LISTEN MODE, SENDING 2 WILL
33 REM- SET THE DM141 TO RANGE 2 (EG 2.0000V).
34 REM-

40 FORI=1TO 500:NEXTI
45 REM- DELAY NECESSARY TO ALLOW DM141 TO SETTLE ON NEW RANGE
50 GOSUB605
55 REM

60 PRINT"DATA STRING FROM BUS IS ";D$ : PRINT
76 REM- THE VOLTMETER READING IS NOW DISPLAYED ON THE PET SCREEN
80 PRINT
90 PRINT"DM141 VOLTMETER READS ";LEFT$(D$,6);" ON RANGE ";MID$(D$,7,1)
91 REM- USE OF LEFT$ STRING FUNCTION IS NEEDED AS DM141 ONLY USES THE
92 REM- FIRST 6 CHARACTERS THAT THE OMNIBUS SENDS. FURTHER PROCESSING
93 REM- IS NEEDED TO CORRECTLY POSITION THE DECIMAL POINT.
94 REM- THIS IS DONE USING RANGE DATA TRANSMITTED AS 7TH CHARACTER.
105 REM- THIS TIME A FURTHER READING WILL BE TAKEN WITH THE DATA-VALID
106 REM- PROTECTION FACILITY, ON RANGE 3.
110 M$="3":GOSUB505
115 REM- SETS DM141 TO RANGE 3
120 FOR I=1 TO 500 : NEXT I
125 REM- DELAY FOR DM141 SETTLING TIME
130 M$="P":GOSUB505
135 REM- SET DATA-VALID PROTECTION MODE
140 GOSUB605: REM- TAKE READING
150 GOSUB805
155 REM- TO SEPARATE PARTS OF DATA STRING
160 PRINT:PRINT"DM141 READS ";V$;" ON RANGE ";R$
170 PRINT:PRINT"NOW THE RANGE INFO IS USED TO PLACE DP":PRINT
180 PRINT:PRINT"DM141 MEASURED VOLTAGE =";V
182 REM
183 REM
185 REM- USING DM141 IN SINGLE SHOT MODE THUS AVOIDING HAVING
187 REM- TO PROGRAMME DELAYS IN SOFTWARE.
190 M$="B"
200 GOSUB 505
205 REM- SETS DM141 IN SINGLE-SHOT MODE
210 M$="4":GOSUB505
215 REM- SETS DM141 ON RANGE 4.

220 FOR I=1TO500 : NEXT I
225 REM- DELAY NECESSARY TO LET DM141 COMPLETE ITS LAST READING,
227 REM- NOT NECESSARY IF WE HAD STARTED THE PROG IN SINGLE-SHOT MODE.
230 M$="A":GOSUB505
235 REM- INITIATES A READING.
240 M$="BP":GOSUB505
245 REM- SUPPRESSES FURTHER READINGS AND SETS
246 REM- THE DATA-VALID PROTECTION MODE
260 GOSUB605
261 REM- REQUEST DATA
270 GOSUB 805

271 REM- POSITION DECIMAL POINT
280 PRINT:PRINT"SINGLE-SHOT READING ON DM141 =";V
290 END
505 REM- THIS SUBROUTINE SENDS THE CHARACTER STRING REPRESENTED BY M$
515 REM- ON THE IEEE BUS TO THE INSTRUMENT WITH LISTEN ADDRESS 8
520 OPEN1,8
525 REM- REFERS PET FILE 1 TO BUS ADDRESS 8
530 PRINT#1,M$
535 REM- PET'S SOFTWARE HANDLES BUS PROTOCOLS TO SEND OUT M$
540 CLOSE1 :REM- TIDIES UP PET FILE
550 RETURN
560 REM
```

```
605 REM- THIS SUBROUTINE RECEIVES DATA VIA THE BUS FROM A TALKER
615 REM- ON THE BUS WITH ADDRESS 8.
620 OPEN2,8
625 REM- REFERS PET FILE 2 TO BUS TALK ADDRESS 8
630 INPUT#2,D$
635 REM- DATA FROM TALKER IS PLACED IN STRING VARIABLE D$
645 REM- AGAIN PET'S SOFTWARE HANDLES ALL BUS PROTOCOLS AUTOMATICALLY.
650 CLOSE2: REM- TIDIES PET FILES
660 RETURN
805 REM- THIS SUBROUTINE USES THE RANGE INFORMATION TO CORRECTLY
815 REM- POSITION THE DECIMAL POINT.
820 V$=LEFT$(D$,6)
825 REM PUTS VOLTAGE PART OF DATA STRING INTO STRING V$.
830 R$=MID$(D$,7,1)
835 REM- EXTRACTS RANGE INFORMATION FROM DATA STRING.
840 V=VAL(V$)*10+VAL(R$)/10+6
845 REM- MULTIPLIES READING VALUE BY TEN TO POWER OF RANGE NO.
855 REM- AND DIVIDES THIS BY 1 MILLION TO GIVE CORRECT VOLTAGE.
870 RETURN
READY.
```

Fig. 3.1   Sample program on P6 Farnell bus introduction (courtesy Farnell)

Other short cuts have also been devised to overcome problems, for example, the lack of output control on the SRQ line by the Pet, and the corresponding absence of the SRQ implementation in the Pet Basic language. In an operating situation a bus transfer may occur when a device tries to signal SRQ (Service Request) to inform the controller to set up the sequence to take readings from the device. A particular solution exists in the case of non-bus devices which are linked to the controller via a bus adaptor or coupler unit whereby the Pet can be programmed to monitor the SRQ line, and upon detection of an SRQ can correctly establish the data transfer sequence.

To achieve maximum data rates with the Pet and with some of the other slower controllers, it is helpful to use machine code instructions rather than the BASIC commands. In the case of an experienced programmer operating a Pet used with a fast systems voltmeter, the use of machine code would give a 5K byte/s rate, corresponding to 625 ASCII readings/s, while Basic coding would only provide 75 readings/s in a character string format. Nevertheless, even this is quite good when compared with a manual operator.

When using the CBM machine its bus anomalies noted previously must be accounted for. Briefly these are that the CBM must be the only controller in the system, that its message delimiter is fixed at 'CR', and that if the connected device is not responsive to 'CR' the END message on the EOI must be used. The REN line is grounded permanently and this is always held 'true'. IFC is not implemented, though after switch-on the IFC line is true for 100 ms. Memory reading and writing statements must be used (PEEK and POKE) for both data transmission over the bus and for the handshake procedure. SRQ is not recognised by the CBM in BASIC but can be implemented via PEEK and POKE, these must also be used in the implementation of the addressed and universal command group. Inserted spaces in the first group of input data are ignored and the following time limitations should be observed. When the CBM 'listens' DAV must go low within 65 ms, and when it 'talks' NDAC must go high within 65 ms, after it has set DAV low. On timeout failure the transfer is halted and the appropriate status word is set. In this example to reduce program length the required memory addresses are labelled A_1–A_3, e.g.:

```
170   A1 = 59426:        REM A1–5 are labels of memory locations
180   A2 = 59427
190   A3 = 59456
200   A4 = 59425
210   A5 = 59424
```

HANDSHAKE PROCEDURE SUBROUTINE

```
640 REM *****************************************************************************
650 REM              SUBR. SOURCE HANDSHAKE                        *
660 REM *****************************************************************************
670 ::
680 POKEA4, PEEK(A4)OR8:                    REM SET DAC=1
690 POKEA3, PEEK(A3)OR67:                   REM SET RFD=1; SET
                                            DAC AND RFD INPUTS=1
700 T=PEEK(A3)AND64:IFT=OTHEN700:           REM WAIT UNTIL RFD=1
710 POKEA2,PEEK(A2)AND(255-8):              REM SET DAV=1
720 T=PEEK(A3)AND1:IFT=OTHEN720:            REM WAIT UNTIL DAC=1
730 POKEA2,PEEK(A2)OR8:                     REM SET DAV=0
740 POKEA1,255:                             REM ENABLE DIO1-8
750 POKEA4,PEEK(A4)AND(255-8):              REM SET DAC=0
760 RETURN
770 ::
780 ::
790 REM *****************************************************************************
800 REM              SUBR. ACCEPTOR HANDSHAKE                      *
810 REM *****************************************************************************
820 ::
830 POKEA5,255:                             REM CLEAR DATA INPUT
840 POKEA4,PEEK(A4)AND(255-8):              REM SET DAC=0
850 POKEA3,PEEK(A3)OR2:                     REM SET RFD=1
860 POKEA3,PEEK(A3)OR4:                     REM SET ATN=0
870 T=PEEK(A3)AND(255-128): IFT=1 THEN870:
                                            REM WAIT UNTIL DAV=1
```

```
880 POKEA3,PEEK(A3)AND(255-2):      REM SET RFD=0
890 B=(255-PEEK(A5)):               REM B=INPUT DATA
900 POKEA4,PEEK(A4)OR8:             REM SET DAC=1
910 T=PEEK(A3)OR128:IFT=OTHEN910:   REM WAIT UNTIL DAV=0
920 POKEA4,PEEK(A4)AND(255-8)       REM SET DAC=0
930 POKEA3,PEEK(A3)OR2:             REM SET RFD=1
940 RETURN
```

To send a universal command, address, or addressed command the ATN line must be true, so the following sequence must be followed, for example, to send an addressed command:

Set the DIO output memory location
Set ATN = 1
Call subroutine—Source Handshake
Set ATN = 0

In the following example a 'start' command is sent to a Philips PM 2527 rms multimeter, using the bus addressed command GET (Group Execute Trigger):

```
CBM GET ROUTINE
360 POKEA1, (255-54):        REM SEND LISTEN ADDRESS
    BOSUB550:                (DEC. VALUE)
370 POKEA1, (255-8):         REM SEND GET (GROUP
    GOSUB550:                EXECUTE TRIGGER)
520 ::
530 ::
540 REM ****************************************************************
550 REM         SUBR. SEND COMMAND OR ADDRESS             *
560 REM ****************************************************************
570 ::
580 POKEA3, PEEK(A3) AND (255-4):
                             REM SET ATN=1
590 GOSUB 650:               REM SUBR. SOURCE HANDSHAKE
600 POKEA3, PEEK (A3)OR4:    REM SET ATN=0
610 RETURN
READY.
```

Note: The addressed command GET is very often used as START command of a device, e.g. in the PM2527.

```
260 T=PEEK (A2) AND 128: IFT=OTHEN 260:
                             REM WAIT UNTIL
270 D=86: GOSUB410:          SERVICE REQUEST (SRQ)
380 ::                       REM SERIAL POLL DEV.
390 ::                       ADDR. 22 (=86DEC)
```

```
400 REM *********************************************************************
410 REM              SUBROUTINE SERIAL POLL                        *
420 REM *********************************************************************
430 ::
440 POKEA1, (255-25): GOSUB550:   REM SEND SPE (SERIAL
                                  POLL ENABLE
450 POKEA1, (255-D):              REM DI01-8=TALK
                                  ADDRESS (D=DEC. VALUE)
460 POKEA3, PEEK (A3) AND (255-4):
                                  REM SET ATN=1
470 GOSUB650:                     REM SEND TALK
                                  ADDRESS D
480 GOSUB800:                     REM SUBR. ACCEPTOR
                                  HANDSHAKE (READ ST)
490 POKEA1, (255-95): GOSUB550:   REM SEND UNT
                                  (UNTALK)
500 POKEA1, (255-25): GOSUB550:   REM SEND SPD (SERIAL
                                  POLL DISABLE)
510 RETURN
```

These examples again demonstrate the operator time consuming
nature of primitive low level software; these commands can be
immediately executed with a full BASIC GPIB controller.

Controller DVM/plotter program (Philips)

In this example the Philips 4410 bus controller commands a DVM,
takes readings and directs them to a vector plotter which has been
directed to write alphanumeric measurement data simulating a
printer. Here the controller talks to the plotter (primary listen address
36, secondary address for character string printing 108), and the
PM 2441 DVM (listen address 54). The controller listen address is 32
(ASCII 'SP') and the talk address is 64 (ASCII '   ').

```
100  INIT                        (Initialisation of the bus)
101  PRINT # #4, 103:            (Initialises plotter)
102  PRINT # #4, 117:            (Initialises plotter)
     0, 2000
110  PWRITE 63,64,36,108,54:     (Characters R9A2F0 are sent to the
     'R9A2F0Ex'                  DVM and plotter simultaneously
                                 using the PWRITE function: 63 is the
                                 UNL unlisten bus command; the fol-
                                 lowing numbers the above instrument
                                 addresses)
111  PWRITE 63,54: 'EEx'         (DVM receives a start measurement
                                 command, the 'E' not received by the
```

<table>
<tr><td>

```
112   PWRITE 63:
113   INPUT # #22: A$

114   PRINT A$
115   PRINT ##: 'H'

120   END
```

</td><td>

plotter since only the DVM was addressed after the unlisten command '63'. 'R9A2F∅ has also programmed the DVM how to measure the voltage. The plotter meanwhile has printed the instruction)

(The measurement made by the plotter is entered on the bus and read by the controller as A$, this displayed on the screen)
(Returns plotter pen to home position)

</td></tr>
</table>

It is worth studying the literature of all the companies for examples of applications and associated software. This information can help greatly in assessing system and device requirements and in helping to solve individual problems.

The German company of Rhode & Schwarz have developed a special version of the Pet designated the 'PPC' which not only has an inbuilt small disc drive store of 80K byte capacity, but also possesses special commands for all bus operations (nomenclature written around the 'IEC' version) as well as an optional RS-232-C interface. Pet limitations are thus overcome and this model represents a welcome addition to the controller range.

Recently two UK companies have produced enhanced CBM Pet machines providing them with full bus capability. Both PMM Ltd. and Datron Electronics can supply versatile low cost bus controllers based on CBM computers. PPM have fitted new firmware giving in addition to full bus control further control oriented commands plus power-on auto load and EPROM program/storage.

The Datron version, called the 1400, is developed from the CBM 4032, and will support the DOS2 floppy disc operating system. A standard GPIB socket is fitted with a rear panel reset button providing a processor and bus reset to help overcome lock-up states while retaining BASIC programs in RAM. An autostart is incorporated which operates in conjunction with the accessory disc store and a number of subroutines are present to carry out proper servicing of the bus including POLL, TRIGGER, CLEAR, LOCKOUT, LOCAL, SRQ and TIMEOUT.

MODULAR CONTROLLER

Of the other examples which are representative of pure controller types, the HP9915 forms a good starting point. A so-called modular

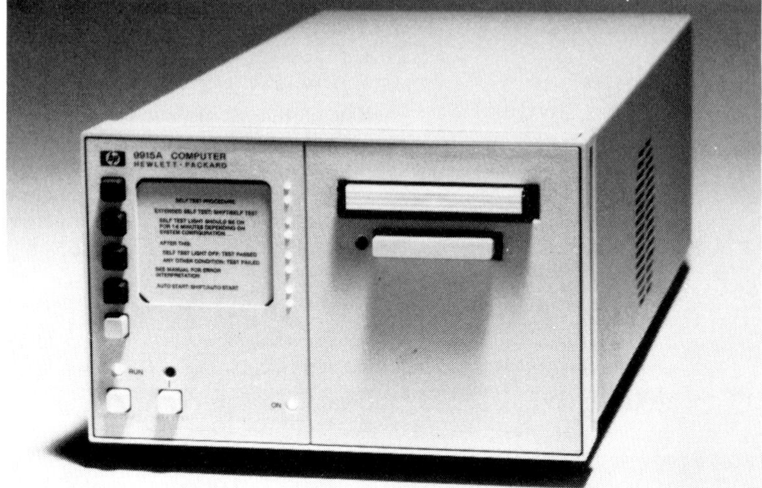

Fig. 3.2   *A modular computer with mass storage cartridge and limited operating controls* (*courtesy Hewlett-Packard*)

computer, it comprises a stand-alone box containing the main works of the HP85 desk top controller with an option of the cartridge program and data storage facility built in, but no keyboard or CRT is present (Fig. 3.2). It has four ('shift' extension to 8) buttons with a mode indicator allowing selection of two test programs and start/stop control. Test pass or fail indication is also given and the test results may be transferred to the optional cartridge store for later computation or documentation as required. The unit has an auto-test, auto-start mode requiring no 'load' commands or similar setting up and thus requires the minimum of operator interaction or skill. The programming may be developed on an auxiliary HP85 controller, here used as an emulator, and the HP85 itself can also serve as a data processor for data on cartridges coming back from a group of modular controllers on a production test line. In concert with its peripherals, this 'base station' computer/controller can, if required, provide statistical documentation on production quality in the form of both graphical and tabular results.

In a similar manner to the Systron Donner 3520, Eprom plug-in boards of up to 32K byte capacity may be installed to provide a fast durable program or software store. Program development hardware to develop the EPROM boards is also available. As with the HP85 the I/O capabilities include interrupt handling to speed bus data transfers, bit manipulation, program control of the interface configuration and easy data formatting. If required a CRT display, custom controls and a full typewriter keyboard may be added, although these would take the system cost well beyond its basic level.

While configured with bus applications in mind alternative data line or interface systems may be used simultaneously with the HP9915, including the RS-323-C, bit parallel and BCD, thereby allowing interfacing with older or simpler instruments. Where high volumes of data need to be stored or perhaps where a fast storage speed is required, a magnetic disc memory should be used. The HP9915 can also be programmed to handle this in conjunction with a mass storage disc unit. It can also print or plot the results in conjunction with a bus or auxiliary interface compatible printer or plotter.

LOW COST GPIB DEDICATED

Still specialised, but with reduced peripheral drive capability the Systron Donner 3520 is a lightweight and compact unit, providing an inexpensive controller function which is fully bus compatible and capable of a number of tasks within its memory capacity. While only 2K of RAM (Random Access Memory) is available inboard, the eraseable PROM (Program Read Only Memory) plug-in of 2K and 4K byte capacity conveniently expand the capacity. To aid pro-gramming this machine carries a special version of BASIC which is orientated to the bus, even to the extent of a number of dedicated keys devoted to important bus controls and commands. The single key BUSIN, for example, transfers data from a selected instrument to the LED, 40-character display line and also into its accompanying input buffer store. An example of its single keystroke programming is given in the following simple program to set a function, range and mode on a bus DVM and take a reading from it. Note, (command), signifies a single keystroke.

```
1Ø   (BUS CLEAR)                ! Interface clear sets known quiescent
                                   state (IFC)
2Ø   (BUS REMOTE)               ! Remote enable (REN)
3Ø   (BUS ADDRESS) Ø 1 Ø 1 Ø    ! Enters DVM address (listener/talker)
                                   into controller
4Ø   (BUS OUT) YSL              ! Selects DVM function (DC), range
                                   (20V) and mode (sample)
5Ø   (BUS IN)                   ! Read DVM measurement into buffer
                                   and display
```

This is clearly a speed advantage over the typical BASIC equiva-lent. A useful accessory provided for the unit is a compact bus status line indicator, showing via an LED array the logic state of the lines. Advanced versions of this device are more accurately specified as bus analysers, such as the 4810 from ICS which allows storage of a limited sequence of bus transmissions (100) and provides step-by-step control to analyse faults present on a bus system. Due to the speed and handshake timing complexity of the bus, conventional logic analysis is unreliable and can be quite slow to undertake. Bus analysis complexity extends up to the Tektronix display formatter, which can write up the bus transmissions in an easily read tabulated form, these decoded from the logic levels and timing on the GPIB (see Chapter 6).

For the Systron Donner controller, while semi-skilled users are probably required as the unit is not foolproof in terms of keyboard masking, it remains one of the least expensive true bus compatible units.

Apple

The APPLE series of 'personal' computers have also been put forward for bus applications and their good quality keyboard and advanced Basic programming have appealed to many users. A GPIB interface is now an option though in contrast to the Pet, neither display nor data storage is built in. By the time an Apple is properly configured for bus use and supplied with the required interface, a CRT monitor plus disc store, the resulting price is rather greater than for a simple Pet, but even so it would still rate as an inexpensive controller. An important feature of both Pet and Apple computers is their world-wide sales and distribution network which has resulted in the production of a wide range of low cost peripherals such as disc storage units and line/graphics matrix printers. With an accessory interface such as the California Computer Systems '7490', a comprehensive implementation of the GPIB is provided by Apple, and in addition a wide range of other interfaces are now available together with appropriate software, though most of this is not bus orientated. More advanced Apple machines will also have optional bus capability.

Adaption of RS232 computer to bus control

In theory any computer with an RS232C interface may be adapted to a GPIB controller form using a sophisticated coupler. For low cost computers the cost of the coupler often exceeds that of the computer and bus compatible versions are clearly the answer. However, where more costly computers have already been installed a 'bus controller'

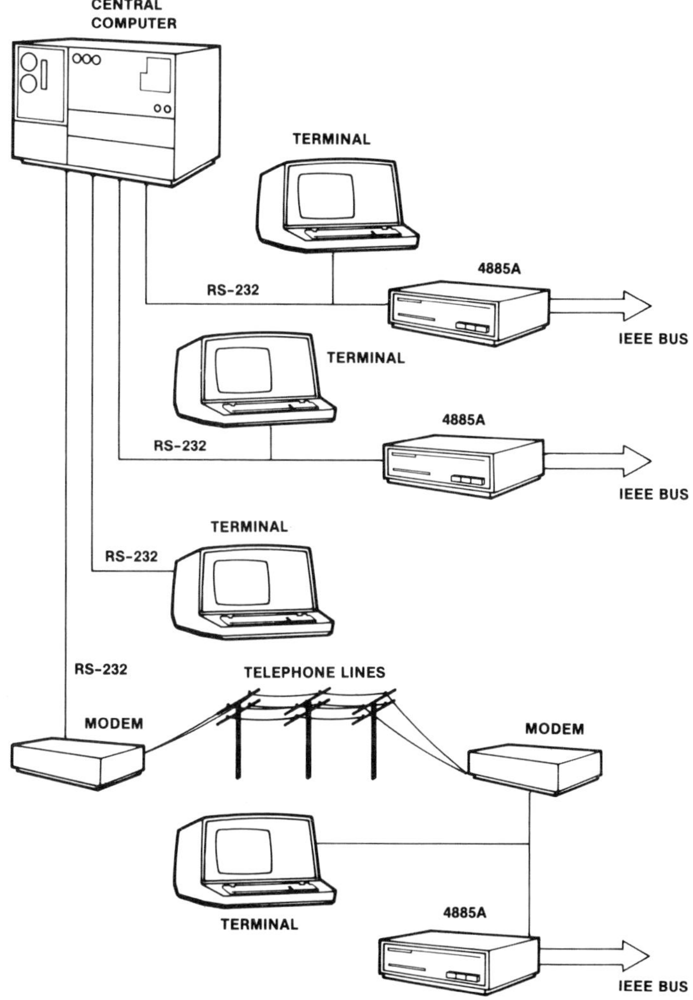

Fig. 3.3(a)   Extension capabilities of a bus adaptor (ICS-488-5A, RS232 to IEEE-488 (courtesy ICS)

adaptor may well prove cost effective for getting the main unit onto the GPIB. ICS quote the use of a Xerox 560 central computer, time shared among a number of terminals and test stations, where controller adaptors provide computer bus operation at specific terminals stations (Fig. 3.3).

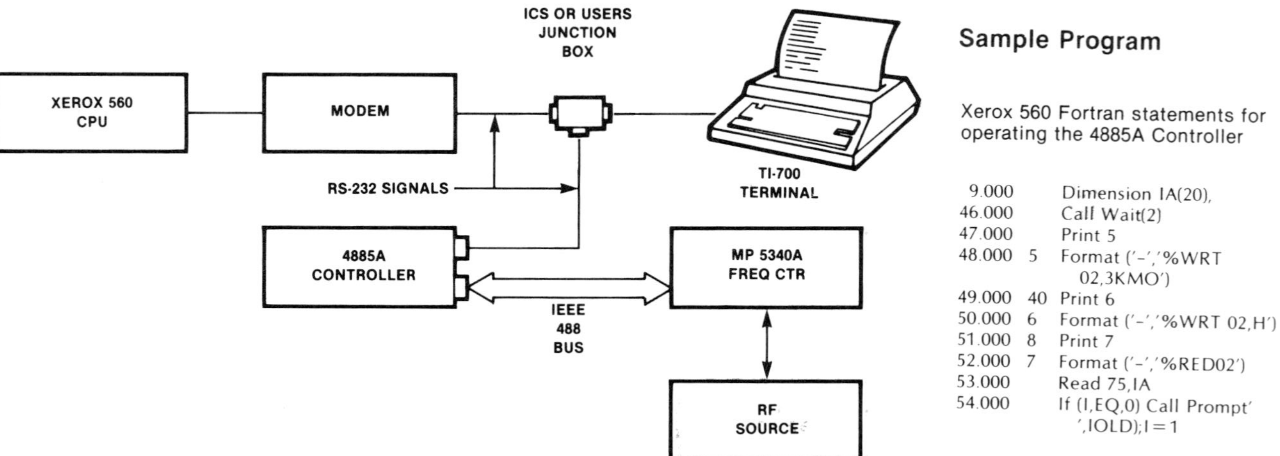

Fig. 3.3(b)   Application of bus adaptor (courtesy ICS)

Sample Program

Xerox 560 Fortran statements for operating the 4885A Controller

```
9.000       Dimension IA(20),
46.000      Call Wait(2)
47.000      Print 5
48.000   5  Format ('-','%WRT
               02,3KMO')
49.000  40  Print 6
50.000   6  Format ('-','%WRT 02,H')
51.000   8  Print 7
52.000   7  Format ('-','%RED02')
53.000      Read 75,IA
54.000      If (I,EQ,0) Call Prompt'
               ',IOLD);I=1
```

MEDIUM COST UNITS

Other relatively moderate cost computers with a GPIB compatibility or optional bus facilities include the ABC 80 from Sweden, the Osborne and the Hewlett Packard 85 and 98 series which when bus configured dominate the middle price range and also extend up to high cost systems. The simplest HP unit is the 9815A, a small calculator-controller operating in Hewlett-Packard's RPN language, but provided with full GPIB control via an optional interface module. This machine carries some convenient inbuilt facilities such as an auto-start sequence together with a small tape cartridge memory store, a Led single-line numeric display and a strip printer, the latter also providing a useful readback of the program lines during development.

Moving into the next price range, the leading exponent of versatile bus control is HPs newest compact model, the HP85 (fully configured as the 85F); which conveniently integrates keyboard, c.r.t. display, fast storage on a data cartridge and a graphics strip printer (Fig. 3.4). Accessory Roms covering a wide range of applications are also available, together with the I/O Rom plus GPIB interface necessary to equip it for full bus control. An extensive range of peripherals and software is building up for this model and it represents a relatively foolproof entry to this manufacturer's range of bus interfaced instrumentation. Programmed in Basic and provided with comprehensive supporting documentation it also offers the emulator role for the modular controller previously described. A version called the 83 is supplied without the thermal printer and cartridge memory store, and this is probably the best choice for the more complex and heavy duty control applications where the greater speed and longer life of a disc store peripheral would score over the tape cartridge or in situations where neither are required.

A notable feature of the HP85 is the inbuilt graphics facilities together with the facility to copy data unchanged from the small inbuilt CRT display straight onto thermal print paper (Fig. 3.5). For small batch production tests, this could be valuable in providing complete and easily understood documentation of the test results on the spot (see Chapter 4, Transceiver test).

HIGHER SPEED 16-BIT CONTROLLERS

Where high data rates or volume are expected and perhaps in addition the controller may also be required to process or compute the data during the test cycle, the smaller 8-bit computers such as

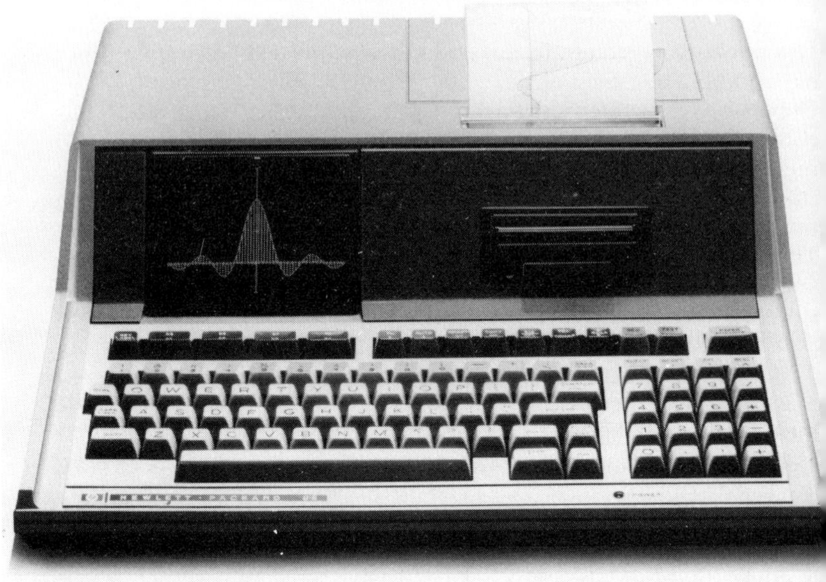

Fig. 3.4 Low cost integrated computer controller, HP-85 (courtesy Hewlett-Packard)

Apple, Pet and HP85 might prove too slow and a faster 16-bit machine may be needed to handle the load. For example, where arrays of points from a spectrum analyser are accessed and processed on a repetitive basis, a 16-bit machine could handle the subroutine in fractions of a second while the simpler controller type would take a minute or two. Where many such sequences are involved in a test routine, the saving in time and money may be considerable with the larger machines. In addition the more advanced controllers will have multi-level operating systems with several layers of interrupt priority as regards the servicing of control lines and units on the interfaces. The HP9825, a 16-bit fast bus controller, has the ability to run a live keyboard, do computations and operate both the display and run the program simultaneously. In contrast with the HP85 series, the latter's CPU (Central Processor Unit) takes on each task individually; driving the bus, reading the keyboard entry, executing the graphics; as program running and processing temporarily blanks out the other functions.

Controller prices can reach a substantial level before reaching an advanced specification, due to the incorporation of enhanced facilities. Systron Donner offer their 3530 instrumentation controller with up to 64K of memory, Basic language and fast 100K inbuilt tape drive (a second drive may also be fitted). In the hands of advanced programmers it can be programmed in assembly code for data speed-up and also offers a RS-232-C port as standard to drive an inexpensive printer or other similar device. A good quality 12-inch CRT display is incorporated.

The US-made Kontron PSI-80 is another attractive enhanced specification controller similarly priced depending on what options are taken up. These comprise a 64K memory with two inbuilt disc drives and the GPIB interface. Fitted with a restful green CRT and a full keyboard this design is based on an 8-bit CPU, namely the ubiquitous Z80, and is unusual in offering the high level language COBOL as an alternative to BASIC.

There are few high level languages that can be used to implement the GPIB apart from ATLAS and its variants and these are costly to run due to the computer size required. By using a low-cost compiler, Racal Automation have developed an ATLAS-based GPIB language called SABRE which is provided on their RAL 2050 controller. A relatively expensive controller based on the 8-bit 6809 CPU, it provides a full-sized 12-inch green VDU, graphics facilities and a built-in dual 7-inch floppy drive by Persci: 256K bytes of test programme store is available, the other drive containing the easily edited and updated compiler and resource library, the key to the system. Highly readable, self-documenting test programs are the result. DMA is provided to the disc stores giving rapid data access. 32K of RAM is specified and the standard software includes the REBATE EDITOR, SABRE COMPILER, UNIVERSAL CONTROLLER, LINK, and PRINT.

At a rather lower price the US company Systel Computers has introduced a bus controller with general-purpose data processing facilities. The model 48 offers two independent GPIB ports, two parallel data ports and an RS232 serial port. The bus ports operate up to 14K bytes/s and two processors a 280 and an 8085 handle CPU and interface functions. The CP/M operating system is included together with a GPIB enhanced BASIC to provide direct bus control commands.

GRAPHICS CONTROLLER

Tektronix are also active in this field and offer the 4051—a relatively inexpensive computer controller using an 8-bit CPU and offering 8K bytes of memory expandable to 32K. It includes a fast tape cartridge store of 300K capacity, being distinguished by its very costly flat-

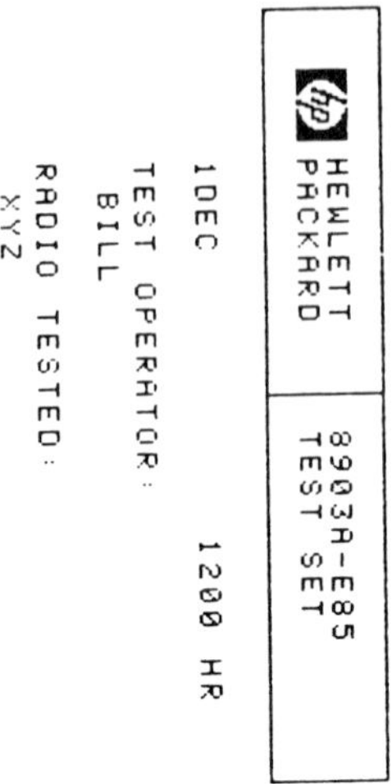

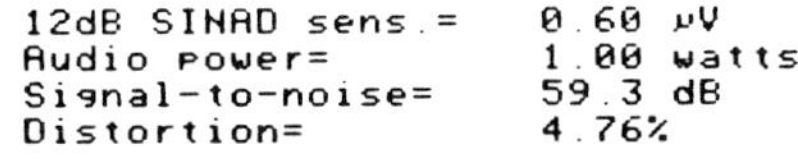

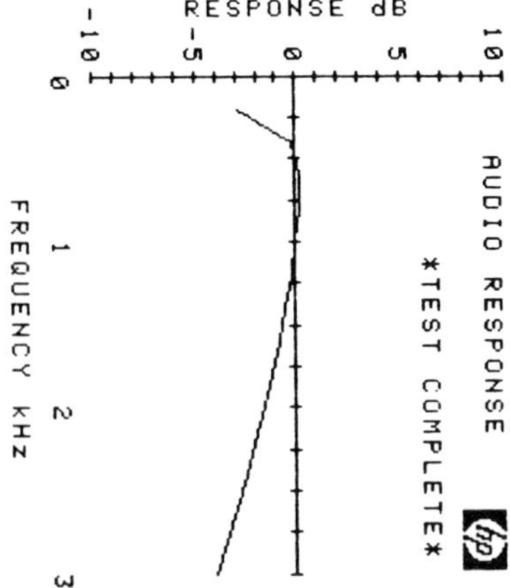

Fig. 3.5   Test system/printout direct from HP-85 (courtesy Hewlett-Packard)

Fig. 3.6   High performance graphics controller, TEK-4052 (courtesy Tektronix)

screen storage CRT which provides excellent non-flicker graphics with close on a 0.8 mega point resolution using a visually unfatiguing green field (Fig. 3.6).

If higher processing speeds are required, the 4052 can be employed, this comprising a 16-bit processor version. This is provided with 32K or 64K of RAM, and is sufficiently powerful to be classed as a general purpose scientific minicomputer in addition to fulfilling its role as a bus controller.

ADVANCED DEDICATED TEST CONTROLLER

A superior type of GPIB controller has appeared which can be programmed taking into account the minimum of operator skill, and which in its basic form simply consists of a bright, clear green CRT display on which all instructions are shown, together with key labels for the appropriate touch sensitive areas on the CRT faceplate. A total of six rows of ten touch locations are provided and they may be pre-programmed and electronically masked so only the 'keys' required at a specific stage are labelled and made available. This FLUKE 1720A is highly dedicated to bus test systems, reflecting this company's

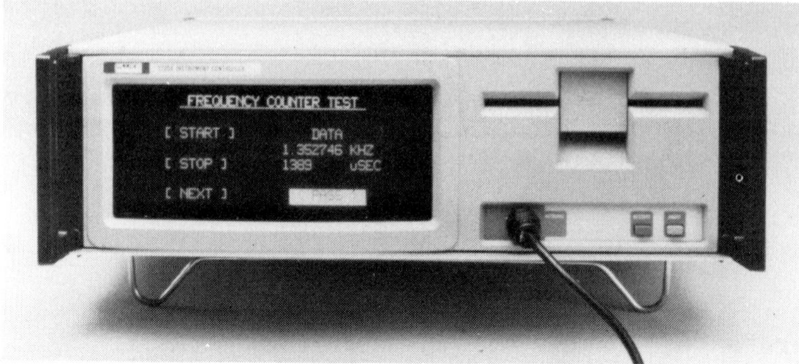

Fig. 3.7   High performance touch screen dedicated controller, 1720A (courtesy Fluke)

strong involvement in bus orientated instrumentation. Two inbuilt mass storage modes are available, a floppy disc offering 175K byte and an optional electrohic simulated disc, providing a highly durable and fast 128K or 256K byte capacity in addition to the live user memory of 60K bytes. A simple front socket provides for ready connection of the supplied keyboard when required for programming, and using a fast 16-bit CPU, the unit also has two each of RS-232-C and GPIB interfaces as standard, the latter allowing system segmentation for faster operation, with up to 28 bus instruments under full control. Well priced for the facilities, i.e., a basic machine with interfaces, the optional electronic memory is, however, quite costly per 128K unit compared with disc but is supremely durable (Fig. 3.7).

Another recent 16-bit processor based computer/controller is the HP9826A. Ostensibly a development of and companion to the HP9825, the '26 in fact owes much to the HP85 in its compact format, containing as it does an inbuilt small CRT monitor, versatile graphics facilities, and a disc drive store. An 8 MHz rate, 16-bit processor provides fast computation, even exceeding the noted HP9825, despite the '26 operating in BASIC rather than the more compact HPL language used for the '25. Other language options including Pascal are available for the '26 and it will undoubtedly be used as a highly versatile and powerful integrated scientific computer and industrial controller. HP features such as electronic keyboard masking can at the same time make it uncomplicated for the less skilled operator to use in test arrangements, removing the chance of errors and making operation quicker and easier via the CRT labelled special function keys (Fig. 3.8).

In some respects the '26 resembles a compact System 9845B, which is the big Hewlett Packard computer controller. Some measure of the

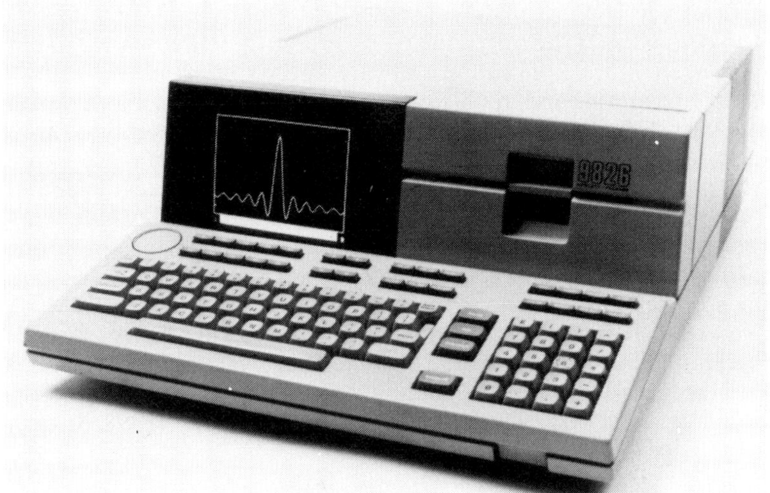

Fig. 3.8   Powerful universal computer controller, HP-9826A (courtesy Hewlett-Packard)

latter's power may be gathered from its user memory expandable from 56K to 500K byte and its 12-inch graphics programmed CRT with a 0.25 mega point capacity. An 80-character wide thermal printer is in-built. A single program line entry can dump the entire screen display including good-quality graphics at high speed (up to 480 lines/min) onto the printer. Two 217K byte cartridge tape drives are included and to speed up programmed system operation up to fifteen levels of priority interrupt may be established. Essentially organised for the Basic language code its programming carries numerous enhancements to greatly extend its powers. The HP9845 pricing reaches the upper range depending on the options and interfaces exercised, but at a lower price the sister model, 835, still offers a decent turn of speed, also with an optional 12-inch CRT monitor, memory up to 256K, Basic programming and a high level of GPIB controller versatility. The 16-bit processor in the HP9835 provides a strong processing power and in addition the option of assembly language programming can maximise the performance of systems employing very high data densities and rates.

With all the Hewlett Packard units a wide range of fairly expensive but excellent quality peripherals are available. The quality of the operating and instruction manuals provided is excellent; this factor alone can save much programming time.

This chapter would not be complete without a brief résumé of the HP9825 itself which is by no means obsolete and continues to provide a strong performance in the controller field. On the programming side it is perhaps less 'friendly' due to its use of the HPL language but conversely much application software already exists in the form of sample programs and application notes, etc. Storage is via the small and fast HP data cartridge providing 250K bytes and the unit includes a user memory expandable to a maximum of 31.4K bytes, while a thermal strip printer is built in, just 16 characters wide but quite sufficient for the condensed HPL language used. Adding to its slightly old-fashioned feel is the alphanumeric strip program line display of 32 LED characters. The machine is, however, fast enough for special I/O (in/out) operation at up to 400K, 16-bit words/s. A live keyboard and direct memory access (DMA) are further notable features and in addition to the bus interface a variety of ROMS and interfaces are available. Fully configured for bus operation, the cost is below the HP9826 which itself comes below the HP9835 (now augmented by the HP9836).

Larger computer installations with GPIB control abilities in the upper price range include the Tektronix 4054, a top class model using a 19-inch CRT and offering high resolution dynamic (moving) graphics, suited amongst other things to structural analysis. The Digital Equipment Corporation LSI-11 is suitable, as are the advanced HP computers such as System 1000, to bus control applications and a high-quality interactive terminal. The HP2649A is also described as a microprogrammable terminal/controller. This costly but handsomely styled unit may be viable for a prestigious custom control system and can be equipped internally with a variety of RAM, ROM and PROM options. Via the modular internal architecture these may be fully programmed by the test system designer to uniquely fulfil the speed and application requirements needed. A fine high-resolution CRT is inbuilt and sophisticated graphics are an optional facility.

After encountering some early bus protocol hangups the (IEC) controller from Philips based on the system 4000 was shelved and the minicomputer was successfully reconfigured as a microprocessor development unit. However, with more recent classifications of the bus specification and Philip's strong involvement with bus com-patible equipment the controller option has now been reintroduced. Called system 4400 this computer controller belongs to the advanced group and is based on a 16-bit central processor with facilities for Basic, assembler and Fortran programming. It has a 12-inch display with inbuilt twin floppy disc stores of 640K bytes and a 64K byte random access operating memory. While graphics commands are pre-set to direct a plotter, at present the screen graphics appear more limited. Many interfaces may be fitted in addition to the bus but it is worth noting that as a European machine it conforms to the IEC version of the specification in its connector plug form. Via thirteen interface slots and a wide variety of analogue, digital, A/D, and voltage programming boards, the 4400 is clearly well suited to process control in addition to a bus system instrument computer. At present this instrument when configured on the bus is relatively expensive.

The established Tektronix controller terminals are large units, this partly due to their bulky graphics storage CRTs. A recent introduction is the 4041 controller, a stand-along modular unit with a small operating keyboard of limited facility. Of high power, based on a 68000 16-bit microprocessor, some 32-bit enhancements are present such as 24-bit addressing. Memory up to 160K byte can be fitted, a magnetic cartridge storage is built in and a 20 character miniature strip printer provides hard copy of numerical data—useful for data logging, for example. Special interface features include two bus interfaces and additionally two RS232. As Tek put it, this allows system speed optimisation by placing the slowest bus devices on one interface and the fastest on the other. The RS232 ports are convenient for peripherals or for communication with a local display terminal or with a host computer.

Other speedup features include three duplex transfer modes, Interrupt, Fast Handshake, and Direct Memory Access. A small portable keyboard may be linked to eight modular controller and operator points and data displayed on a twenty-character LED display on the controller faceplate (Fig. 3.9). Designed as part of a new integrated approach to instrumentation based on the established Tektronix TM500 instrument system, the latest generation of this system being fully bus compatible. A simplified English-like code format has been developed for the system by Tektronix to aid programming, which the following example illustrates.

A function generator is to be set for a 10 MHz triangle wave output at 2.1 V. A typical code would run:

CI F10E6A2.1

Triangle code   Frequency 10^6 Hz   Amplitude 2.1 volts

Tektronix's 'Engineering English' would give

FUNC TRI; FRGQ 10E6; AMP 2.1

allowing easier reading of the program at a later time.

Fig. 3.9   Rack test system integrating modular controller, 4041 (top left instrument of rack) (courtesy Tektronix)

CONSIDERATIONS FOR CONTROLLER AND SYSTEMS PURCHASE

The following categories apply:
- (1) ownership
- (2) application
- (3) specification
- (4) implementation, and
- (5) growth allowance.

Ownership issues include cost; the total cost must include software development not just the controller hardware, and must also include considerations of reliability, serviceability, supplier commitment and backing, warranty, maintenance contracts and a contingency plan in case of prolonged failure. An assessment of the quality of the company organisation backing a device is vital; if necessary visit the company's service facilities.

Finding out whether the proposed system meets the required application begins with a detailed specification for a prototyped test procedure. Considerations will include controller memory, data transfer rates, system timing requirements, human interface requirements, facilities for peripherals and what peripherals may be needed, graphics data entry method, operator interference safeguards such as control masking, plus worked solutions available for some or all of the proposed tests. Professional help may be needed to choose the controller, particularly if the manufacturer has not adequately specified his product; for example, in terms of a detailed conformance with the bus message groups, data rate speeds, available storage and program capacity or has not shown representative examples to illustrate execution speed on the bus. In the case of an instrument, the front panel commands may be fully executable on the bus. The availability of applications engineers from the supplier is a consideration and also when pricing the package, allowance for sufficient memory should be made as memory restrictions can greatly complicate and slow programming.

The implementation, setting up and use of a bus system must also be planned, these aspects including operator choice, availability, their skill level, and training if so required. Subsidiary factors such as the quality of the manuals supplied with the equipment, including up-to-date amendments, may be vital if future personnel are to keep the system running smoothly. Error trapping and bug detection facilities are valuable as are bus analysers in various forms. The 'friendliness' of the software and hardware interfaces is a major factor, and the worth to the customer of the associated software increases in proportion to the ease of learning, programming and maintenance. To maximise forward compatibility proprietary languages should be avoided where possible.

Finally, some consideration should be given to the future growth of a test system. Purchase of a bus controller may only be a small specialised acquisition for a particular duty but the likelihood is that the decision will be the foundation of a program of test automation based on bus systems in which a large investment of company capital and time will eventually be made. Allowance for such growth at the planning stage will influence the controller purchase and ideally it should be capable of versatile expansion in many areas of performance and bus capability. As every experienced engineer knows, the purchase of a versatile high performance device rarely ends at the application for which it was first specified. New applications are readily found once the product's abilities become familiar.

4

Controlled systems and software examples

INTRODUCTION

A bus system may be planned comprehensively or may just grow, with units added as and when the need arises. However, a coherent instrument purchase policy on the part of a company is worthwhile. For example, if a gross proportion of its electronic instrumentation is GPIB compatible it may then be used flexibly to build bus controlled systems in different company areas at different times, thereby providing maximum equipment utilisation.

If an instrument breakdown occurs another different unit available may be pressed into service and the system program quickly modified to allow its insertion.

It must be stressed that maximum exploitation of the GPIB relies on the understanding and utilisation of its reliability, convenience, programming speed, universality and flexibility. These aspects are crucial to the rapid setting up of inexpensive automatic or semi-automatic controlled test systems at short notice, suited to development, prototype and small production batch checking, particularly where the devices under test (DUT) are specialised and relatively complex. Where high speed or high unit volumes are encountered dedicated high performance ATE and control is superior.

The bulk of this chapter is comprised of examples of bus systems with a selection of controller types and program samples or excerpts which should be of particular help to newcomers to this field. However, before these are presented some illustrations of the power of a computer controller are included to show how it may enhance the performance and add to the functions of costly digital equipment.

INSTRUMENT ENHANCEMENT VIA GPIB CONTROLLER

The controller/computer can take data from instruments and readily manipulate or process it. For example the 1/3 octave analysed readout on a digital spectrum analyser is often displayed on screen with a 60 dB or 80 dB dynamic range scale factor. Suppose an enhanced resolution was required for more critical analysis. Generally the 1/3 octave data readouts from such analysers are to 0·1 dB resolution; it is a simple matter to modify a program which transfers data from the analyser to the controller and thence to the plotter, so that any desired scale factor or magnification may be set on the final plot, or on a constructed display on the controller VDU, thus adding a magnification function.

Where frequency weighting would be applicable for frequency response data this can be entered into the computer program as an equation or as an array of scale factors versus frequency, which can then be applied under program control to the data input. Numerous other possibilities also exist; for example, the mathematical manipulation of results on a statistical basis. Two sets of data corresponding to two response curves may be summed or subtracted, and the result graphed for inspection. The possibilities are almost endless for such data manipulation.

Enhancement of HP3582A analyser

Where versatile instruments are concerned, perhaps with the capability to output data in several forms from different memory stores, a controller can be used in special ways to speed up data transfers and to obtain useful data from inside the analyser system which would otherwise be inaccessible to the instrument alone.

The HP3582A analyser is a good example of a 'systems' instrument using the bus, where a considerable range of valuable enhancements are possible via programmed interaction with a suitable bus controller.

The basic instrument comprises a 20 MHz to 25 kHz fast Fourier digital spectrum analyser, operating with a linearly spaced frequency axis of 256 line resolution. By suitable controller programming the instrument may in addition be directed to produce a 1/3 octave band, logarithmically spaced display over the full audio bandpass. This is achieved via a software routine which directs the instrument through the bus interface to analyse the bandpass in three frequency span stages. This is done in order to store enough detail in terms of line density to compute digital filter equivalents of the ANSI standard 1/3 octave bands. Suitable weighting and shaping functions are present in the programme, and when the required response has been calculated it is transferred in the appropriate format back to the analyser for display on its own CRT, complete with relevant alphanumeric annotation (Fig. 4.1).

A similar multiple pass, programmed analysis may be used to generate logarithmic 'continuous' spectra from random or pseudo-random noise excitation of the device under analysis.

Both these enhancement programs extend the use of the instrument into the conventional log scaling framework used generally for data presentation in the audio field.

Using the 3582A other performance extensions are also possible via the bus. Direct access may be gained to the internal memory register, allowing the user to extract the information for post processing. Alternatively a time or transient record from an accessory store, possibly captured by a wider bandwidth transient recorder, may be read into the analyser and subjected to the FFT process for display, thus enhancing the frequency range (Fig. 4.2).

Controller instrument packages

The controller enhancement of some instruments is so great that certain versatile test units comprise a bus linked combination of instrument and controller sold as a package, this including comprehensive ready-to-work software. A noteworthy example is the HP8582A automatic high frequency spectrum analyser which comprises a 9825A computer controller, a 8566A spectrum analyser (0.1 MHz to 22,000 MHz), and the 85861A software PAC (Fig. 4.3). With the addition of a printer, automatic documentation is provided and a digital vector plotter will add document quality graphic records if required. The programs are ready recorded on fast data cartridges for immediate use and are organised in such a way that the users may extract chosen subroutines, and develop their own measurement programs as desired. Called 'subprograms', these are held in a 'library' section of the data cartridge.

These routines cover a wide variety of functions including optimum frequency range selection, peak signal recognition, special unit scaling dBV, dBm, etc.; calculation of noise bandwidths, plus digital plotter instructions for log and linear scaling grids and alphanumeric annotation.

The main programs include automatic measurement of harmonic distortion via summation of harmonics, spectrum search, amplitude modulation measurement and noise/impulse bandwidth calibration. This type of comprehensive software backing for elements of a bus controlled system can be invaluable in saved programming time to the purchaser. It is thus essential that the equipment buyer thoroughly researches all of the available software options and

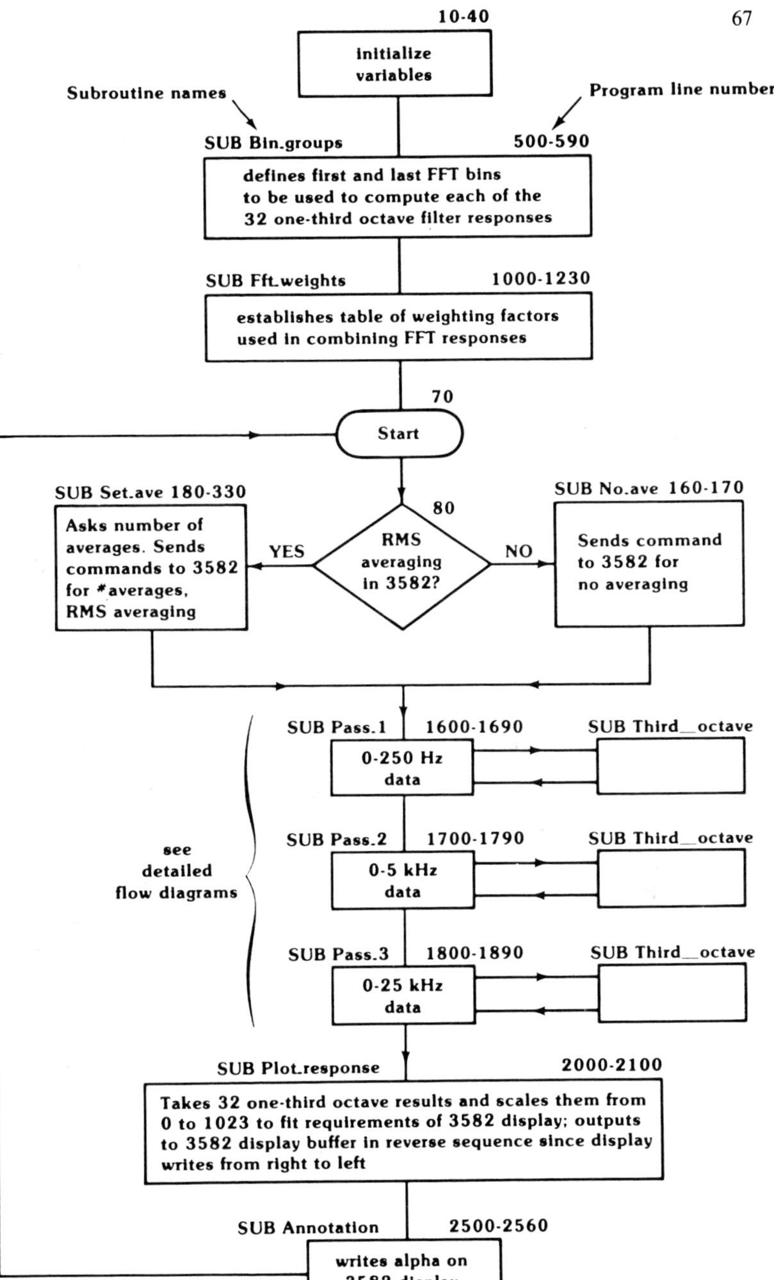

Fig. 4.1 Main flow diagram, $\frac{1}{3}$ octave program for HP-3582A under bus control (courtesy Hewlett-Packard)

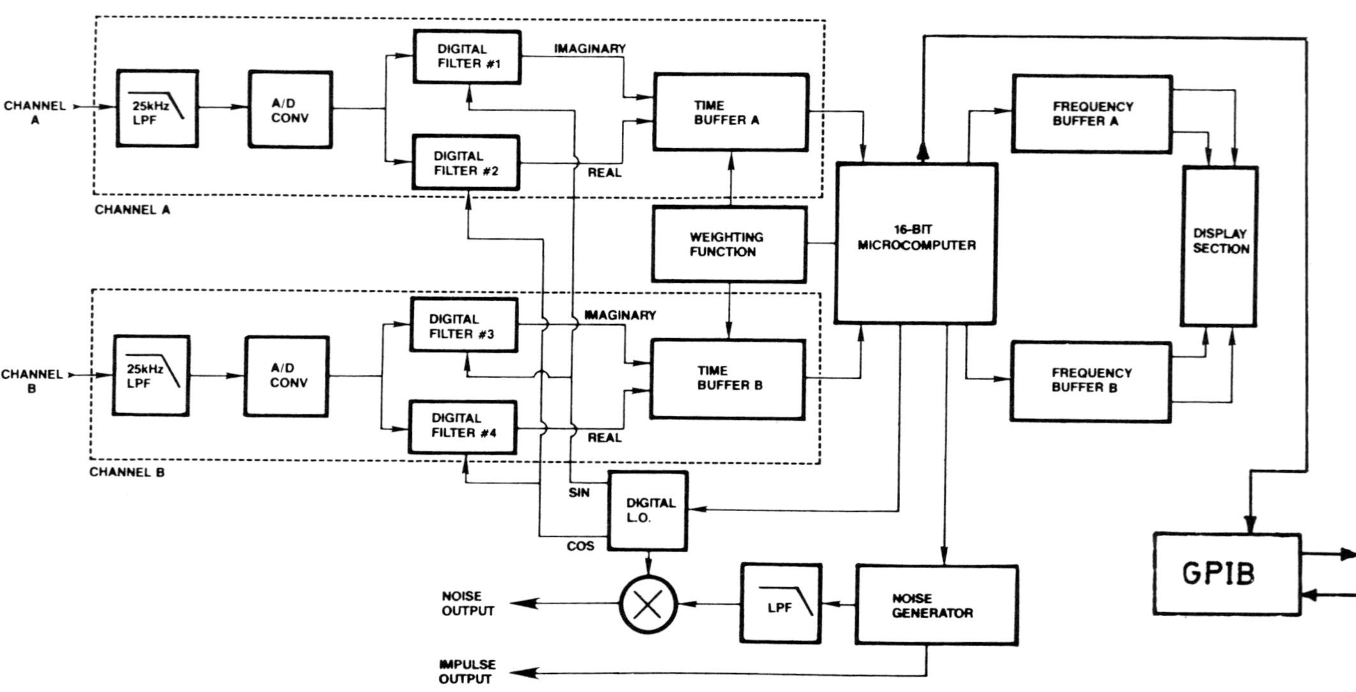

Fig. 4.2   Internal architecture of HP-3582A bus controlled spectrum analyser (courtesy Hewlett-Packard)

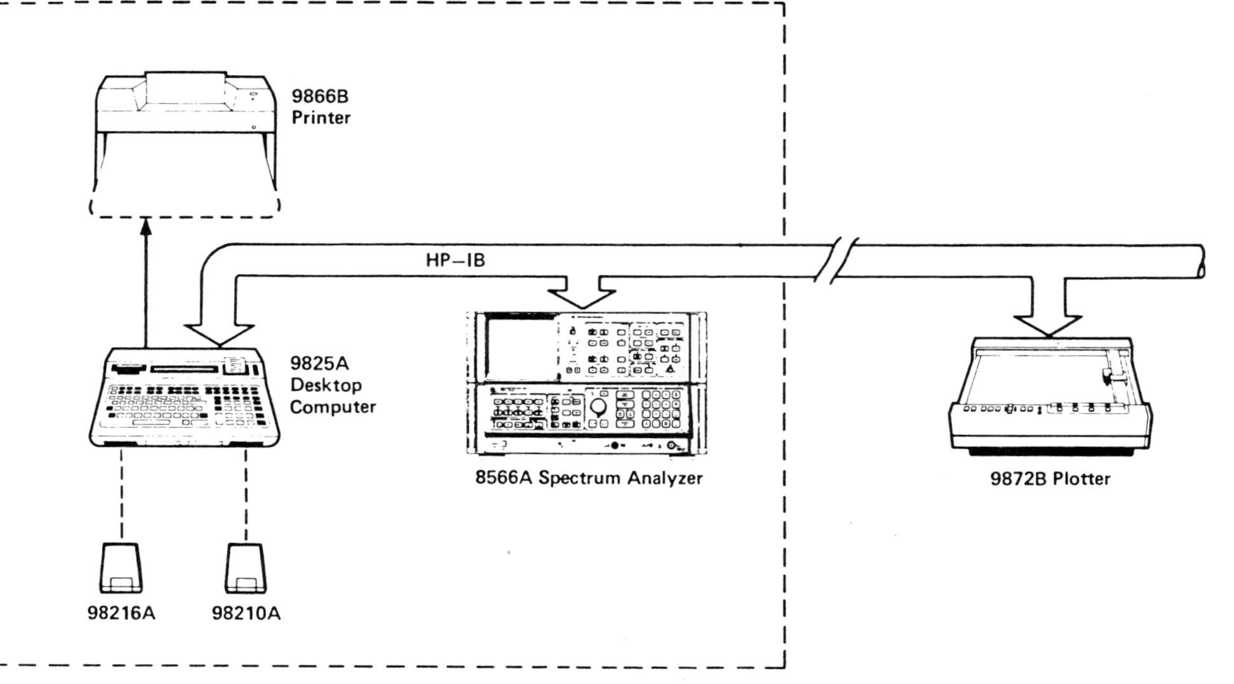

Fig. 4.3   Automatic spectrum analyser configuration (courtesy Hewlett-Packard)

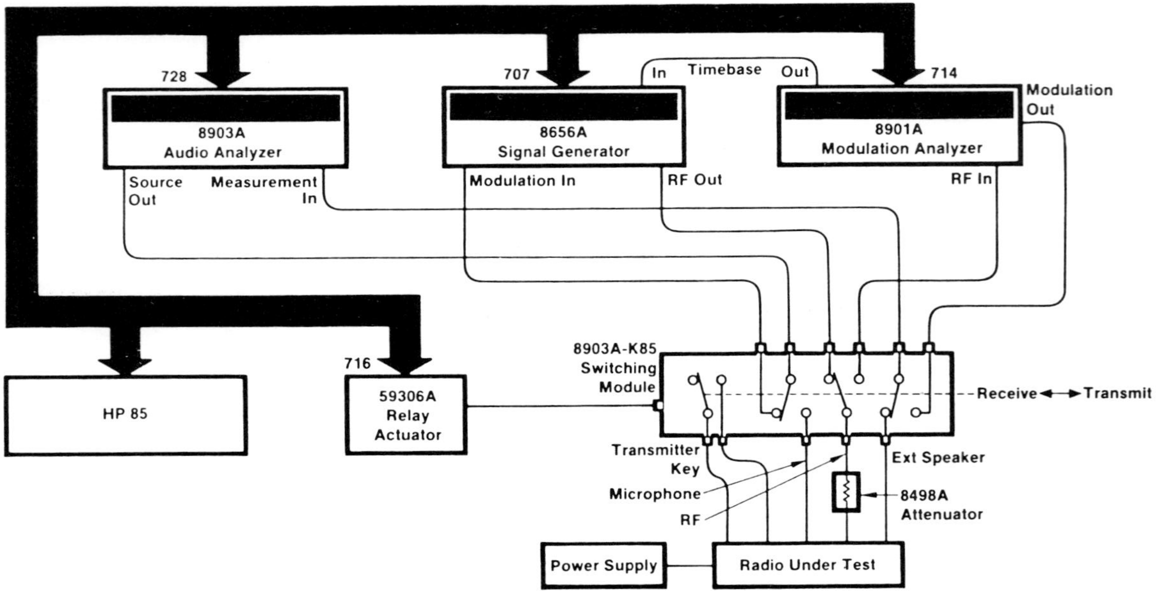

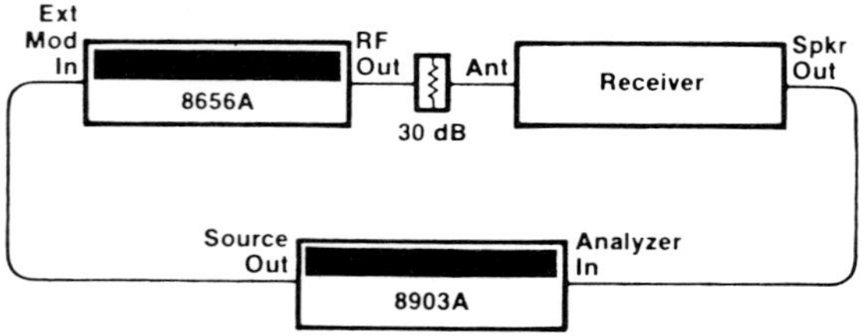

Receive configuration.

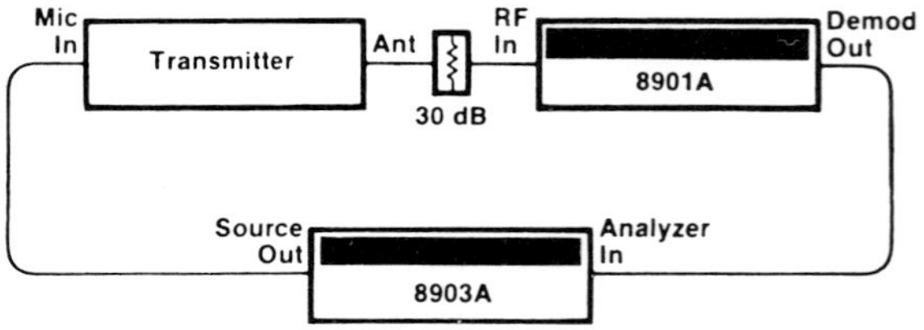

Transmit configuration.

application notes relevant to the controllers as well as the field of application of the equipment to be put on the GPIB.

Transceiver test

Transceiver testing represents a classic arrangement requiring a large array of equipment as well as a skilled and conscientious operator. In general the DUT (device under test) must meet strict regulations and offer an accurate and well specified performance on a number of difficult to measure parameters.

Hewlett-Packard have assembled a comparatively inexpensive test set developed via use of the HP85 moderate cost controller (option 'F'), called the HP8903A–E85 (Fig. 4.4). Essentially it consists of a GPIB controlled RF generator (8656A), a modulation analyser (8901A), an audio analyser (8903A), a simple switching unit and the HP85 with software PAC. With relatively little operator skill, this unit can test a transceiver in approximately one minute, with all data printed out and the response graphed (see Fig. 3.5).

Versatile subroutines allow relatively easy access to many parameters such as checks for DC offset on signal lines and selection of amplitude or frequency modulation modes. Also falling under the classification 'GPIB controller enhancement', the versatile HP8903 audio generator/analyser may be programmed for extra functions such as the generation of fast multiple frequency tone bursts, as used for some telephone dialling systems and for multi-channel selective call radio communications systems. Complementing this enhancement, this analyser may also be set in a fast count mode whereby such tone burst sequences emanating from a transmitter may be measured, transferred at speed to the controller and then displayed.

The following are two subroutines associated with the 8903A analyser.

8903A SUBROUTINES (SOURCE)

```
3000 ! 8903A INST SUBS – SOURCE
3010 !
3100 FRQ(A),kHz                            Set audio frequency in kHz
3110 IMAGE 'FR'DD.4D,'KZ'          Image for 8903A source frequency
3120 OUTPUT 728 USING 3110; A
3130 RETURN
3140 !
3200 ! LEV(A),dBv–600Ω                    Set audio level, dBV EMF.
                          Note: 8903A source has 600 Ω impedance
3210 IMAGE 'AP',3D.DD,'DV'              Image for 8903A source level
```

```
3220 OUTPUT 728 USING 3210 ; A
3230 RETURN
3299 !
3300 ! SOURCE ONLY                      Display source settings
3310 OUTPUT 728 USING 999 ;          10.SP = display settings;
     '10 SPT3'                                    T3 = trigger
3320 RETURN
3330 !
3400 AF SOURCE OFF                   Set audio amplitude to 0
3410 OUTPUT 728 USING 999 ;            (not possible in dBv)
     'AP0 MV'                   AP0MV = amplitude 0 millivolts
3420 RETURN
3499 !
```

8903A SUBROUTINES (ANALYZER)

```
4000 ! 8903A INST SUBS – MEAS
4010 !
4100 ! ACV(A)                             Measure ac rms level
4110 OUTPUT 728 USING 999;                     M1 = ac level;
     'M1T 3'                        T3 = trigger with settling
4120 ENTER 728 ; A                          A will be in volts
4130 RETURN
4140 !
4200 ! DIST(A),%        Measure harmonic distortion, notch method
4210 OUTPUT 728 USING 999 ;                  M3 = distortion;
     'M3T 3'                        T3 = trigger with settling
4220 ENTER 728 ; A                        A will be in percent
4230 RETURN
4299 !
4300 ! SINAD(A),dB          Measure SINAD using notch method
4310 OUTPUT 728 USING      M2 = SINAD; T3 = trigger with settling
     999 ; 'M2T 3'
4320 ENTER 728 ; A                           A will be in dB
4330 RETURN
4399 !
4400 ! S/N(A),dB      Measure S/N ratio, switching 8903A source
4410 OUTPUT 728 USING      S2 = S/N ratio; T3 = trigger with settling
     999 ; 'S2T 3'
4420 ENTER 728 ; A                           A will be in dB
4430 RETURN
4499 !
4500 ! WATTS(A,Z),        Measure equivalent power into load = ZΩ
     WATTS,LOADΩ
4510 IMAGE '19.',3Z,'SPT3'         19.NNN SP = watts into NNNΩ
4520 OUTPUT 728 USING 4510 ; Z   Set NNN = value specified by Z
4530 ENTER 728 ; A                          A will be in watts
4540 RETURN
4599 !
```

```
4600 ! DATA(A)              Make another measurement (except frequency)
4610 OUTPUT 728 USING 999 ; 'T3'          T3 = trigger with settling
4620 ENTER 728 ; A                         A will be in same units
4630 RETURN
4699 !
4700 ! AF CNT(A),Hz                        Count audio frequency
4710 OUTPUT 728 USING 999 ; 'MIR     M1 = ac volts (fastest mode);
     LT3'                            RL = left display (frequency)
4720 ENTER 728 ; A                            A will be in Hz
4730 OUTPUT 728 USING 999 ; 'RR'             RR = right display
4740 RETURN
4799 !
4800 ! HP/BP(A)                     Set HP/BP filters, A = 0, 1, 2
4810 IMAGE 'H',D                Convert values to codes H0–H2
4820 OUTPUT 728 USING 4810 ; A
4830 RETURN
4899 !
4900 ! DCV(A)                              Measure dc level
4910 OUTPUT 728 USING 999 ;                   S1 = dc level;
     'S1T 3'                          T3 = trigger with settling
4920 ENTER 728 ; A                            A will be in volts
4930 RETURN
4999 !
```

Digital multimeter calibration

Proper quality verification for high performance digital multimeters
is time consuming and prone to error, and thus much of the cost of a
given installation is taken up by the precision calibrator (e.g.,
PPM/Rotek 610). A low-cost GPIB controller (Commodore Pet) plus
versatile software (e.g., PPM 'Compucal') can automate the operation
for less than the cost of the calibrator alone. The software program is
held on floppy discs and incorporates 'learning modes' whereby a
complete test sequence may be programmed via simple on-screen
operator prompts, this process typically taking around 20 minutes.
Up to 130 instrument sequences may be stored and during the
running of any given response the operator is given comprehensive
prompts to fully calibrate the DUT. Test data is automatically
printed out and a further optional refinement comprises an 'inventory
store' whereby a test inventory and library of past performances may
be kept, each data disc is capable of holding test information for up
to 2,000 instruments.

A form of 'computerised handbook' may be entered and the
location of adjustments, etc. on the DUT may be illustrated on the
controller CRT. While a direct time saving for the system over a

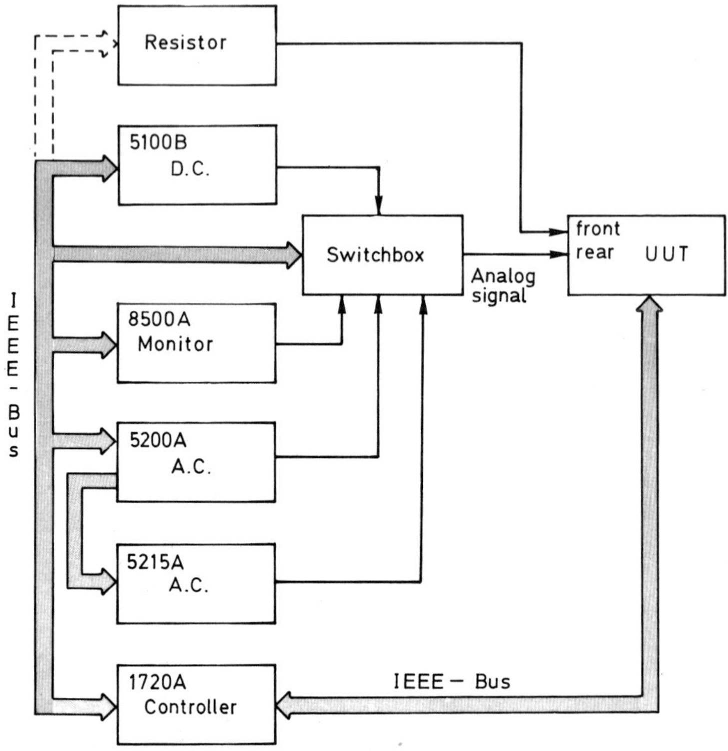

Fig. 4.5   Calibration and test system (courtesy Fluke)

skilled operator is not significant, indirect savings in skill, repeatability, and documentation make it well worth considering.

Fluke have also developed a bus test system for precision DMM calibration. A GPIB controlled switchbox allows connection of various test sources, under the command of the 1720A touch screen controller. Here the DMM is itself under bus control and its range settings for test and calibration are also automatically programmed (Fig. 4.5).

Using a master DMM to monitor the system the inclusion of $\pm 1°$ temperature environmental control for the master endows the entire test set up with a remarkable DC accuracy of just 10 ppm. The switch box is an adaptation of their GPIB translator, the 1120A, and via simple BCD data bus interfaces this can also couple up to three low-cost digital instruments onto the bus while at the same time retaining individual addressibility on controller command.

Selection of a precision SOT (select-on-test) component

An interesting problem has been described by PPM Ltd., concerning the selection of a resistor value for a particular instument's Zener diode reference circuit in order to provide it with a zero temperature coefficient. Conventional trial and error methods necessitated waiting for an environmental chamber to stabilise at the several temperatures required so as to assess the temperature coefficient achieved. When repeated, as was often required with several trial resistor values, it could take days to achieve the required accuracy for each instrument.

An automatic solution was found at a comparatively low cost employing a Pet controller, the PPM 8000 bus scanner/switching unit, a precision voltage reference and an inexpensive DVM, the latter used optimally in null mode to achieve maximum resolution.

The scanner power relays were used to activate the oven temperature settings with the latching relays employed for the selection of the test resistors, thus forming a programmable resistance box. The remaining switch facilities were used to direct the appropriate signals to the null DVM, and sufficient facilities were present to simultaneously handle four DUTs. For each DUT a range of resistors numbered from 1 to 10 were tried at two programmed temperatures and the output voltage measured and stored in the controller. Time was allowed for complete thermal stabilisation and by computation the controller then indicated to the operator the ideal value to attain the zero temperature coefficients. This was fitted by the test engineer and the completed instrument subjected to a check run. In total some 2 hours was found sufficient to complete four instruments and with relatively low volume production the investment in this simple bus interfaced test unit was recovered in under six months as set against normal production costs.

Testing of complex cable harnesses

Where high volume cable forms are concerned dedicated test units are common, but in the case of complex low volume harnesses, such as those used for aircraft wiring with up to 200 lines and several plugs or sockets, a different solution is required. Individual programming to test each cableform for continuity, pin coding, insulation and resistance is necessary, with multiple connections often requiring considerable time.

By using a special switching module for the 8000 GPIB scanner, PPM devised a program which would learn the whole pattern of a given type of correct master harness connected for test. Having stored the characteristic it could then test the samples by reference to the stored data. A Pet (32K with dual floppy disc drive) or an HP85 (useful for its inbuilt fast data cartridge drive and small printer) can both be used to control the system. The test and/or learn time is approximately four minutes. The latter compares with a manual error-prone test time for this type of around 4 hours. A small extra investment would allow an expansion of the set-up to 500 node cables and yet the fast learn multiple cable type versatility would still be retained.

GPIB control of a transient recorder (Datalab's DL920 by Tektronix 4050)

The high resolution graphics and inbuilt data cartridge store of the 4050 are useful adjuncts to a fast transient recorder and the electrical interfacing is comparatively foolproof via the bus. However, some of the difficulties which may occur in data transfers are illustrated by this combination. For example, each memory in the recorder is 4K bytes long and may be transferred on a slow point by point basis via a simple program.

```
100 WBYTE @ 64+4        This specifies the recorder, device '4'
110 FOR I=1 TO 4 Ø 96   in TALK mode via the command and code 64.
120 RBYTE X             FOR-NEXT loop to step through the 4,096
130 PRINT X             data points, enter each one into the
140 NEXTI               controller, display the point.
150 WBYTE @ 95:         UNTALK command to recorder
```

If the whole waveform is required for processing, storage in the controller should be done via an array. However, 4051 controller Basic requires 32,786 bytes to store one 4K time record, which is beyond its maximum 32K byte RAM capacity. A solution to this problem involves packing up to 4 data point values into each array element. Thus a 4K time record could be compressed into a 2K array, thereby fitting comfortably into the controller memory, e.g.:

```
100 DIM A (2Ø48)        Dimensions array for 2K byte
110 WBYTE @ 64+4        TALK command to recorder
120 FOR I=1 TO 2Ø48     Transfers data from
130 RBYTE B, C          recorder packing
140 A(I) = C*256 + B    into 2K byte array—A(2Ø48) using a
                        FOR-NEXT Loop
```

```
150 NEXT I
160 WBYTE @ 95:                    UNTALK command to recorder
170 FOR I=1 TO 2046                Loop to print reconstructed points.
180 PRINT A(I)−INT(A(I)/256)*256;INT(A(I)/256);
190 NEXT I
```

(The lines 170 to 190 recover the separate points from the array for display.)

The following sample program reads a time record from a DL920 recorder and plots it on the entire CRT graphics display area.

```
100 WBYTE @ 64+4;                  TALK command to recorder
110 PAGE 2048                      Sets up the
120 WINDOW 0, 0, 256              graphics window
130 AXIS 2048/16, 16              for the plot
140 FOR I=1 TO 2048
150 RBYTE x 1
160 DRAW I, X1
170 NEXT I                        Reads and plots points
180 MOVE 0, 0
190 WBYTE @ 95
200 RETURN
```

The HP9825 controller uses a condensed form of BASIC called HPL and the following comprises a sample sub-program for point-by-point transfer and display from one recorder memory using a 9825.

```
0 : For I=0 to 4096
1 : RDB(708)→A: RDB(708)→B
2 : A/256+B→C
3 : DSPC
4 : Next I
5 : RDB(708)→A
```

Line 1 is an implicit Read Byte and Bus Address (708) command, splitting the 10-bit recorder point into the 8 bit + 2 bit required for transmitting over the 8-bit IEEE 488 data bus.

Line 2 reconstructs the point as the variable C which is then displayed in line 3. The last line (5) is present to reset the recorder to its quiescent display mode.

Use of the string operation ROM for the 9825 will allow fast I/O (in/out) operations using arrays and removes the need for such subroutines to augment the transfers.

COMPLETE AUDIO TEST SYSTEM

Recent introductions to GPIB controlled instrumentation have now supplied the hardware needed to construct a comprehensive audio analysis system. Low distortion sinewave generators ($-95\,$dB) such as those from Khrohn-Hite or as provided in more comprehensive test sets such as the HP8903 and the Radiometer RE256 are fundamental elements. A second oscillator is worthwhile for intermodulation duty and since the low distortion specification may be relaxed here it could usefully be a wider range (1 Hz to 1 MHz) unit such as a function generator ($-60\,$dB). These generator outputs may be fed singly or in combination, via a programmable switch-box, to the unit under test, with or without appropriate pre-emphasis as would be required for the RIAA disc equalisation (Fig. 4.6).

The switch-box provides a number of facilities from source combination selection to a number of test loads for power amplifiers. On the measuring side, discrete instruments may be employed such as a dvm for measurement of power, related voltage level and dc offset, while a frequency counter allows checking of source frequencies and may not be required if these are well defined. For visual monitoring several options are possible. Programmable oscilloscopes are becoming available which may then be included in the overall system and automatically ranged and scaled. A specialised auto ranging monitor scope is a viable concept for the comparatively limited amplitude and frequency range encountered in audio. In fact, the HP1980A bus controlled oscilloscope incorporates just such a feature, and need not be GPIB interfaced in this respect. However, in view of its 100 MHz bandwidth and high accuracy specification, this application would represent an audio overkill and some of the moderate bandwidth digital oscilloscopes could prove more suitable for bus controlled test installation.

A total harmonic distortion analyser is a prerequisite for audio analysis, and these are now usually automatic and internally programmed for convenience. The notch filtered output from the analyser may be further processed by a Fourier spectrum analyser for harmonic analysis or this instrument may operate directly on the raw signal, for example, in the case of intermodulation analysis. Programmability of the two intermodulation sources and the analyser allows the latter to maintain synchronism and output the readings of required intermodulation products to the controller via the bus.

The test combination provides some useful surprises. For example, measurement of amplifier rated power requires that the input level be gradually raised to a specific distortion point, e.g., 1% total harmonic.

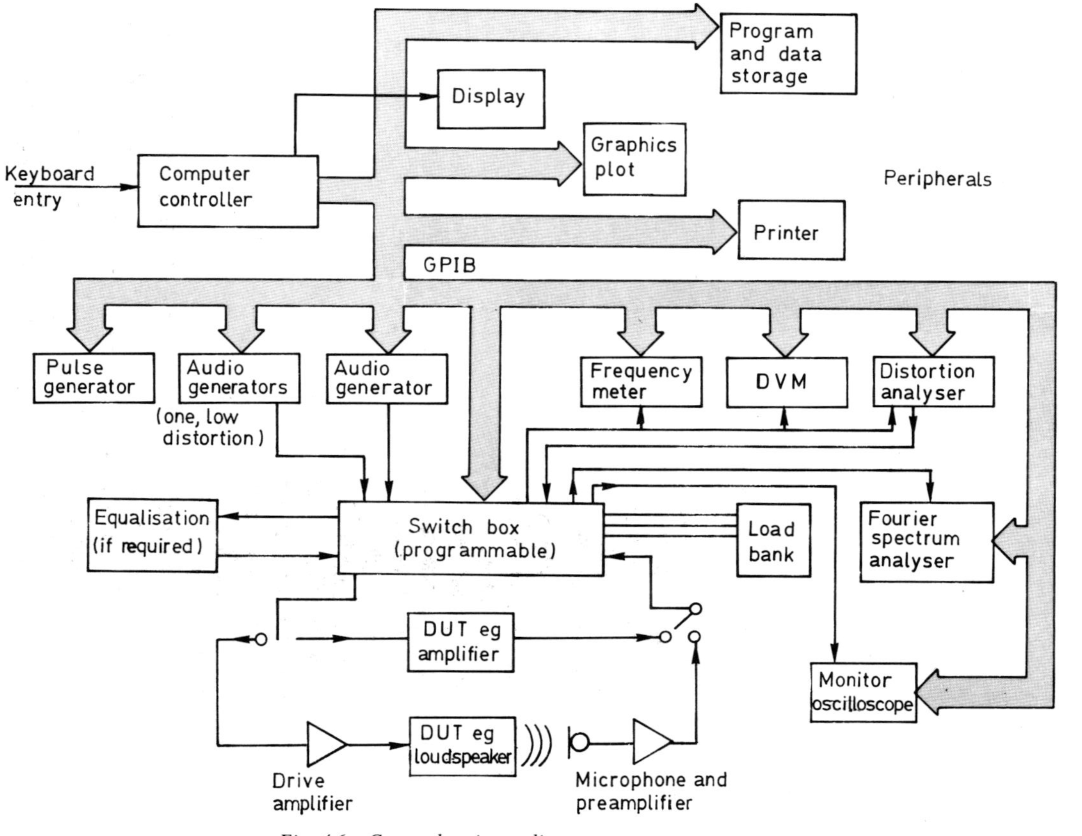

Fig. 4.6   Comprehensive audio test system

This may easily be achieved employing an interactive routine, via the controller program, linking the programmable generator and the distortion analyser. While the recorded power equivalent voltage is measured across the load, the load value is programmed and the voltage may be readily computed to display and print the true power. Further subtleties such as a subroutine operating at lower output power levels to assess the noise contribution to a given distortion reading (total harmonic distortion is the rms sum of the harmonics and noise) may also be incorporated. One method would involve locking the settled auto-range settings of the distortion analyser by controller command and then setting the input stimulus to zero. Alternatively, the results of a previously run signal to noise ratio measurement routine could be recalled and the computer then instructed to compare and assess numerical distortion levels and their validity.

In addition to stepped 'swept' frequency/amplitude response measurement, the programme could also be arranged to provide response figures between calibrated limits ± 0.2 dB or $+0, -3$ dB; these referenced to the usual 1 kHz or any other desired frequency.

The versatility offered by the computing power of the controller may be used in many ways. Mention has already been made of a pre-emphasis or equalisation block in the system diagram. This, of course, could be present as a mathematical equation or alternatively as an array of reference points, and the amplifier characteristic may be compared with the reference to show any errors. Special weighting curves for noise measurements or for psychoacoustic weighting of distortion harmonic spectra are also possible.

Stereo operation is of course permissible using a GPIB switch-box or a similar multi-channel input and output connection unit. Indeed, the various source inputs of an amplifier may also be accessed, although in this case manual mode selection of the required input on the amplifier itself would still be necessary, since this is not programmable.

Some specialised audio instruments on the bus are exceedingly versatile and may incorporate a number of the units separately represented on the audio system diagram. The Radiometer RE256 is a plain box, plus display, containing highly comprehensive audio processing sections plus one- and two-tone signal generation. The HP8903A has many basic facilities including a low distortion generator, a frequency counter, an AC/DC voltmeter, an auto ranging auto tracking distortion factor section, SINAD, and signal to noise ratio functions providing a great saving in numerous separate GPIB links, addresses and signal path interconnections.

The overall possibilities are almost limitless and cannot be fully

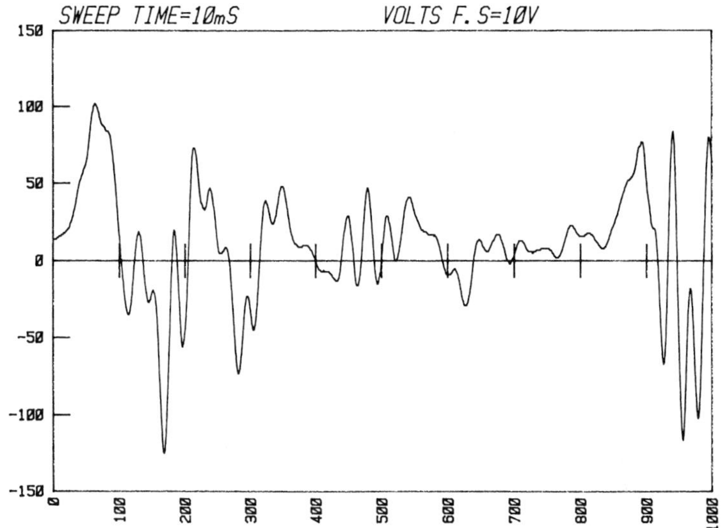

Fig. 4.7   Example of alpha-numeric and graphic printout on bus control vector plotter. Recorded on DL901, graphics by HP-85 and 7225 plotter (courtesy Electroplan)

explored here, but the peripherals suggested in the system diagram are worth noting before moving on. A digital vector plotter will provide annotated reproduction or even hard copy of numerical data and more particularly response graphs, charts and diagrams. A disc store unit would allow rapid accessing of the sub programmes which can be selected from a 'menu', and will also provide permanent storage of the results. Where the alphanumeric output is considerable a fast printer would be appropriate, and despite their moderate line quality a number of these have a worthwhile graphics ability and are inexpensive.

USE OF OTHER INTERFACES

While the bus is clearly the dominant interface, others may be useful in a given set up where one or two simpler or older instruments need to be pressed into service. Most controllers can handle several interfaces and a useful example of this is an HP85 used in conjunction with a Datalab DL901 transient recorder, the latter fitted with an RS232 option, outputting a time record on hard copy via the bus interfaces HP7225 digital vector plotter (Fig. 4.7).

A program listing is given (courtesy Electroplan Ltd.) together with some remarks concerning the program.

```
 11 CONTROL 10.4; 26
 20 ON KEY # 1, "DATA" GOTO 50
 22 ON KEY # 2, "PLOT" GOTO 140
 30 CLEAR @ KEY LABEL
 40 GOTO 40
 50 OPTION BASE 1
 51 ON ERROR GOSUB 400
 60 DIM L(1024)
 70 ASSERT 10; 1
 80 FOR J=1 TO 1024
100 ENTER 10 USING "#, K'; L(J)
115 DISP L(J)
116 NEXT J
120 ASSERT 10; 0
130 OFF ERROR
140 PLOTTER IS 705
150 BEEP @ BEEP
160 DISP "LOAD PAPER & BLACK PEN;
    PRESS 'CONT' WHEN READY"
170 PAUSE
180 FRAME
190 LOCATE 20, 120, 20, 90
200 FRAME
210 SCALE 0, 1000, −150, 150
220 LAXES 100, 50, 0, 0, 1, 1, 5
221 BEEP @ DISP "CHANGE PEN COLOUR
    TO GREEN PRESS 'CONT', WHEN READY"
222 PAUSE
230 PLOT 1, L(1)-128
240 FOR K=2 to 1024
250 PLOT K, L(K)-128,-1 @ NEXT K
260 BEEP @ BEEP
270 DISP "TYPE IN VOLS F.S SETTING
    & PRESS 'END LINE'"
280 INPUT A$
290 DISP "TYPE IN SWEEP TIME SETTING
    & PRESS 'END LINE'"
300 INPUT B$
301 BEEP @ BEEP "CHANGE PEN COLOUR
    TO BLUE PRESS 'CONT' WHEN READY"
302 PAUSE
310 MOVE 10, 155
320 DEG @ CSIZE 5, 5, 15
330 LORG 1
```

```
340 LABEL "SWEEP TIME="; B$
350 MOVE 500, 155
360 LORG 1
370 LABEL "VOLTS F.S=", A$
371 MOVE 10, −180 @ LORG 3
372 LABEL "PRESENTED BY ELECTROPLAN TEL 0763-41171"
373 MOVE 10, −200 @ LORG 3
374 LABEL "Recorded on DL901,
    Graphics by HP-85 & 7225 Plotter"
380 GOTO 20
390 END
400 BEEP @ DISP "INPUT BUFFER
    HAS OVERFLOWED"

410 DISP "WAIT UNTIL D901 CAN
    BE REARMED"
420 DISP "THEN PRESS 'RESET' &
    'RUN' ON HP-85"
430 STOP @ RETURN
```

Line 11	Writes the control byte to the interface control register select code 10 (RS232) register 4, byte = 26.
12, 13	Assign labelled subroutines for entering 'Data' or 'PLOT' to the special function keys of the '85, numbers 1, and 2.
60	Dimensions the data input.
70 to 130	Sets up a loop to sequentially transfer data points from recorder to computer, line 100 refers to an image for the data transfer '#, K' specifying a variable in free field format with the end-of-line sequence at the end of the statement suppressed.
140	Addresses plotter on bus interface at 5.
180–200	Positions and draws a frame for the graph.
210–220	Scales and draws axes.
230–250	Plots data points reading them out of the 'L' array set for the transfer.
270–300	Enter calibration data via keyboard.
310–374	Positions labels, commands 'label' mode, adds calibration data and writes labels.
400	Error trap message.

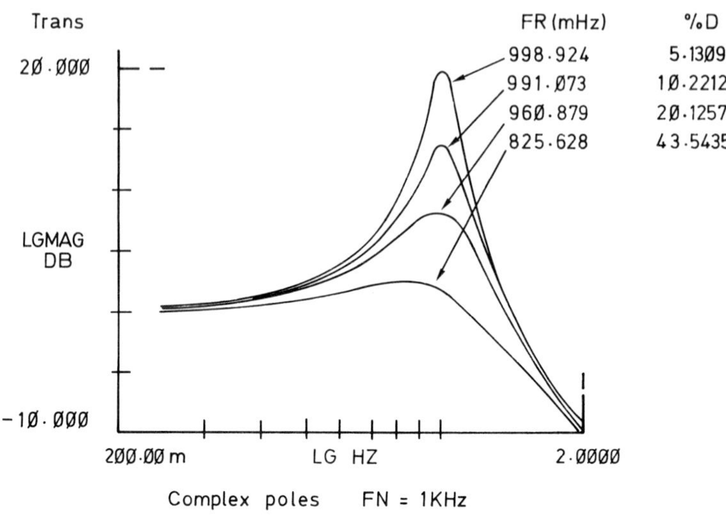

Fig. 4.8 Intelligent analyser drives digital plotter without controller: specimen graphs (*courtesy Hewlett-Packard*)

CONTROLLER OR INSTRUMENT COMMAND?

The distinction between controller and instrument is not always as clear cut as the bus specification might suggest, and in some systems conflicts may occur concerning who or what is actually in control— the operator, the instrument or the controller. Take the case of a micro-processor operated instrument fitted with a bus programmable front panel. In 'local' mode the operator may manually enter settings on the front panel keys for entry to the micro-processor and execution within the instrument. However, if the controller is connected it can do the same thing, and the operating program for the system needs to resolve such anomalies. The bus message LLO (local lock-out) disables the front panels in appropriate instruments and, likewise, release of the REN line allowing 'Remote ENable' can restore manual panel operation. The latter is normally used except where it may be necessary to have both remote and manual control simultaneously available to increase flexibility. Any resulting ambiguities may be resolved by visually assessing the instrument settings via the front panel condition or, alternatively, by the controller interrogating the instrument via transfer of the device dependent message carrying the code for all the internal instrument settings.

Some instruments are also sufficiently intelligent to act as controllers in a limited capacity. Certain HP analysers (HP5420A) have nternal storage and processing to learn and run automatic test programs of an applied nature and may also include permanent software to command a vector plotter via the bus, thereby providing hard copy output. In such an application, a controller may not in fact be required to complete the test installation (Fig. 4.8).

5

Instruments, peripherals and the bus

IMPLEMENTATION

Implementation of the bus in an instrument requires some fairly substantial processing power on the part of the interface board. Before the availability of the more recent microprocessors and specialised bus interfaces integrated circuits, a bus 'card' could be a costly and complex unit in its own right, often more expensive than the instrument itself.

An early discrete talker/listener interface required some forty integrated circuits, even though a number of these were quite complex medium scale integration types (Fig. 5.1). This type of interface operates in conjunction with a microprocessor unit to provide the control software programming for the instrument itself. Subsequently great strides have been taken towards the further integration of the bus interface, resulting in a factor of ten or more reduction in the number of integrated circuits involved. Single chip devices are now available carrying virtually all the responsibilities of the interface, though the least expensive reduce the 1M byte/s maximum data rate.

This interface development is particularly important in the case of the less sophisticated instruments which do not incorporate a microprocessor in their design; in this case the interface card must handle the relevant programming. Generally the specific software is carried in EPROM dedicated to that instrument.

Datalab's model 2000 recorder is just such an example, where the use of the CMOS-based Philips HEF47380V, a microprocessor independent large-scale integrated circuit, has provided a relatively simple interface (Fig. 5.2).

At a somewhat higher chip cost Fairchild have introduced the 96LS488. This takes advantage of the 1978 bus specification amendment which incorporated low power Schottky logic standards and in consequence this chip claims a full bus handshake data rate of 1 MHz. Other manufacturers are also busy in this field including Intel, Motorola and Texas Instruments.

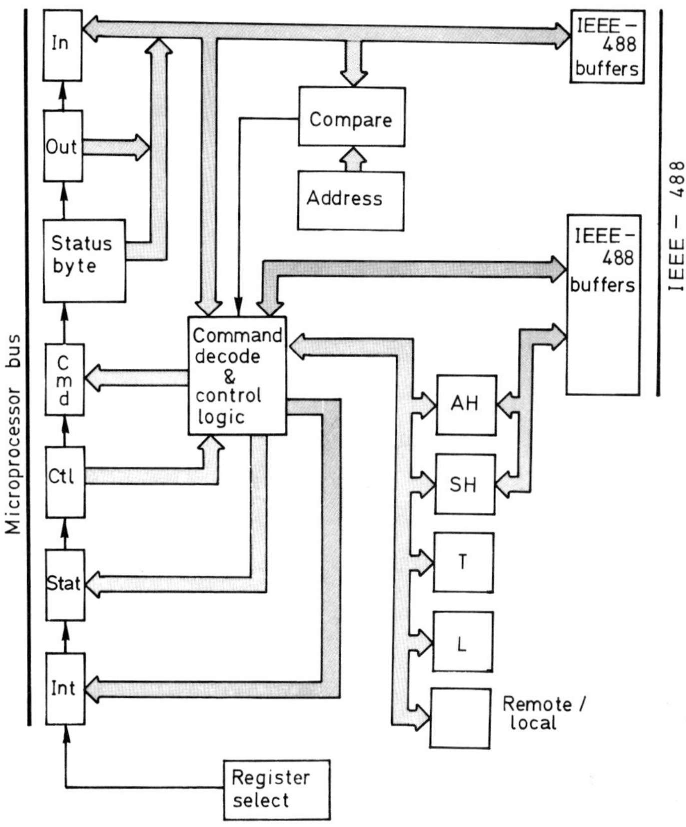

Fig. 5.1   Discrete logic bus interface (a talker/listener interface required about 40 small and medium scale integrated circuits in 1977), (courtesy Hewlett-Packard)

Such developments are all helping to realise the bus system goal of complete interfacing conformance irrespective of instrument cost or origin.

Role of the bus interface in design

While it is certainly possible, and indeed has been done, the retrofitting of a GPIB interface to an instrument is a complex task beset with problems. Often these have been left for the customer to discover with a considerable cost penalty incurred in debugging the operating system. With digital instruments it is logical to design them

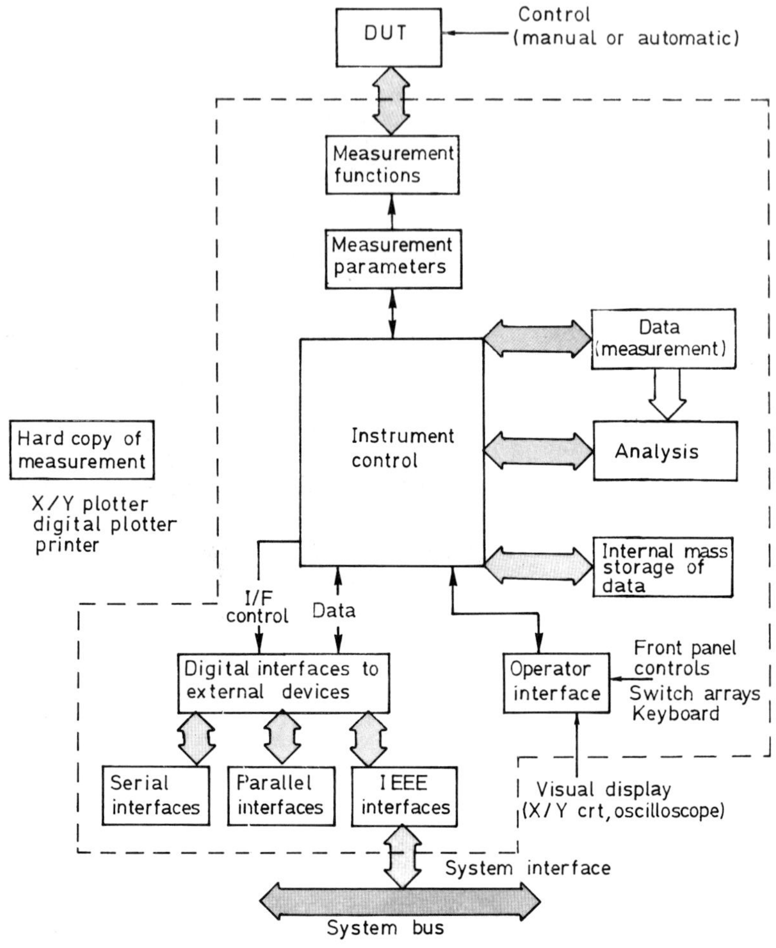

Fig. 5.2   Functions of a generalised bus instrument (courtesy Datalab)

from the outset with GPIB interfacing in mind, even if the feature itself is an option on the final product. Benefits include a guarantee of proper bus implementation if the interface itself is so capable. Certainly software and hardware errors are not unknown even with interface integral circuits from major manufacturers and every designer should be on his guard and check in detail the performance of the proposed interface design according to the full standard specification. At least one manufacturer has discovered that the benefit of GPIB function control of the DUT, or instrument under test, is so great that all units have the bus interface installed during manufacture, enabling a detailed and cost effective bus controlled final test. After testing the instrument, the interface is removed and provided as an optional extra.

The incorporation of microprocessor internal control in modern test instruments has often aided the provision of a bus facility though the main purpose was for reasons of performance enhancement. For example, consider the case of an output attenuator on a precision wide-band signal generator. Frequency dependent attenuation errors are inevitable, degrading the precision. Microprocessor control allows an internal instruction set held on PROM, which is derived by speedy automatic calibration against a reference, to determine the ratio settings of the attenuator at the set frequency to give a higher accuracy of output level. Other features can be readily provided, such as automatic self checking and calibration, and the organisation of complex groups of controls into simple mode controls, thereby simplifying operation and removing front panel facilities which have no direct influence on the instrument operation. With the inbuilt microprocessor some of the bus interface complexity can be reduced, as the micro can take some responsibility for this.

Thus, in a circuitous way, the complex instrument benefits from a bus controlled automatic test system, and further benefits if it is itself a bus controlled design.

BUS IMPLEMENTATION

The interface fitted to a device must be capable of three different function groups and their particular relationships will largely determine the extent to which it conforms with the full GPIB standard. The groups are:
  (1) remote message transfer
  (2) remote message decoding and
  (3) interface functions.
For example, the Philips HEF4738 integrated circuit for bus interfacing incorporates remote message decoding and all interface functions except control and system control; it does not include extended talker or extended listener facilities (Fig. 5.3(a)). In use, a message transfer circuit with driver/receivers plus a switch/shift-register, clock and power-on circuit will be required, and for polling some modification to the message transfer circuit will be necessary (Fig. 5.3(b)). This IC provides the following interface functions (as in the IEC recommendations).

90

The signals to and from the HEF 4738 are:

I *pon*	Input power on	O *red*	Output ready for next shift cycle	I EOI	Input End Or Identify
ICP	Input clock pulse	I ATN	Input Attention	I DAV	Input Data Valid
I *sr*	Input shift register	I IFC	Input Interface Clear	I RFD	Input Ready For Data
		I REN	Input Remote Enable	I DAC	Input Data Accepted

O SRQ — Output Service Request
O DAV — Output Data Valid
O RFD — Output Ready For Data
O DAC — Output Data Accepted
O *ta* — Output talker active
O *sp* — Output serial poll
O P_1–OP_3 — Output Parallel Poll Respond Messages
O PP — Output Parallel Poll Message Enable
O RQS — Output Requested Service
I DIP — Data Input
O *dcd* — Output don't change data
I *nba* — Input new byte available
O *dvd* — Output data valid device
I *rdy* — Input ready for next message
O *trg* — Output trigger
O *clr* — Output clear
O *loc* — Output local
I *cats* — Input controller active or transfer state
O *tct* — Output take control
V_{dd} — Positive Supply line
V_{ss} — Negative Supply line

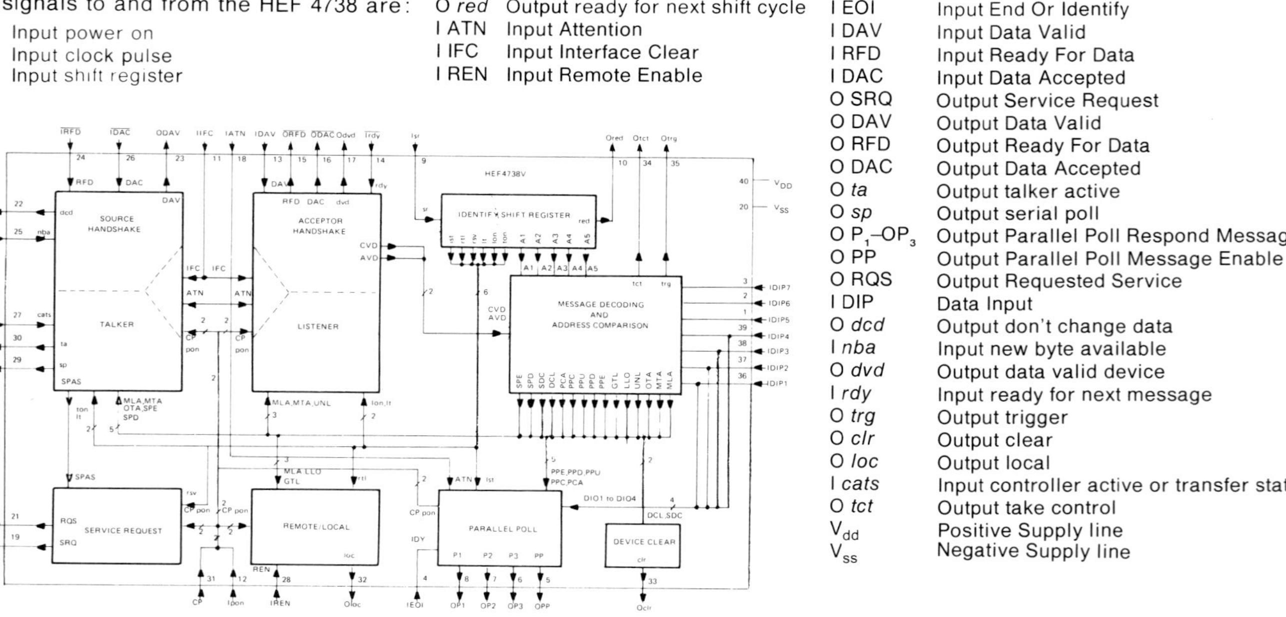

Fig. 5.3(a)   HEF-4738 block diagram (courtesy Grimberg)

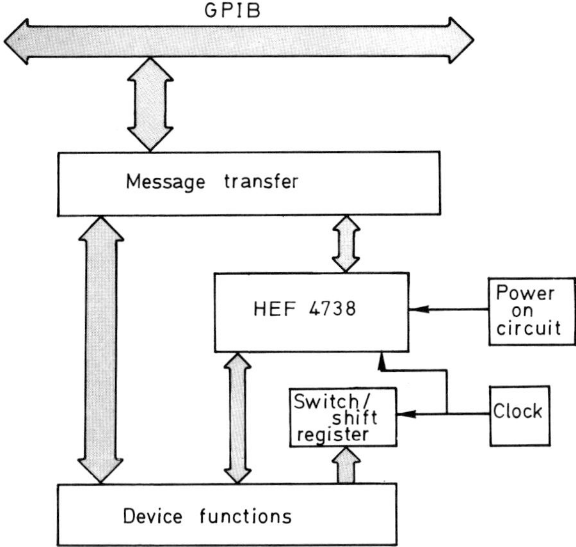

Fig. 5.3(b)   Bus interface structure using HEF-4738 chip (courtesy Philips)

AH1	Acceptor Handshake	Subset 1
SH1	Source Handshake	Subset 1
DT1	Device Trigger	Subset 1
DC1	Device Clear	Subset 1
RL1	Remote/Local	Subset 1
SR1	Service Request	Subset 1
PP1	Parallel Poll	Subset 1
T1 or T5	Talker	Subset 1 or 5
L1 or L3	Listener	Subset 1 or 3

Message decoding

MTA	My Talk Address	Addressing talker
MLA	My Listen Address	Addressing listener
OTA	Other Talk Address	Unaddress talker
UNL	Unlisten	Unaddress listener

Commands executed are

SPE	Serial Poll Enable	Serial polling
SPD	Serial Poll Disable	
DCL	Device Clear	Device clear
SDC	Selective Device Clear	

GTL	Go To Local	Remote control
LLO	Local Lockout	
GET	Group Execute Trigger	Device trigger
PPC	Parallel Poll Configure	
PPU	Parallel Poll Unconfigure	
PPE	Parallel Poll Enable	Parallel polling
PPD	Parallel Poll Disable	
PCG	Primary Command Group	
TCT	Take Control	Control function

Examining the block diagram for the integrated circuit (Fig. 5.4), the chips use positive logic with positive potential while the bus is of course negative logic with a positive potential. The message transfer unit, typically an MC3441, incorporates driver/receiver circuits with the required inversions and appears between the interface and the bus (Fig. 5.5).

Microprocessor based GPIB interface

Motorola's older MC68488 chip cannot operate without the backing of a microprocessor unit, generally a 6800 device, and like the HEF 4738 it requires a message translator/inverter to couple to the bus. The accompanying microprocessor unit requires complete machine code programming for the unit to implement the bus specification and this will require development by a skilled programmer on a microprocessor software development facility (Fig. 5.6).

Single chip interface

Fairchild's 96LS488 is a single chip bus interface which provides a comprehensive implementation and undoubtedly represents a major step in the application of the bus to a wide variety of less expensive instruments. A product of advanced digital logic technology, it employs Schottky TTL in a massive LSI array capable of sinking 48 mA on its output terminals and yet typically drawing under 200 mA overall from a single 5 V power supply. It is ready programmed to interpret and decode bus messages and commands and is supplied in a 48-lead package 2.4 in long by 0.6 in wide.

Together with complete source and acceptor handshake logic it provides fixed or separate talk and listen addresses with secondary addressing also possible. Lacking a controller capability it implements the talk, listen and talk/listen requirements. The source handshake delay is programmable and serial poll, parallel poll, sync

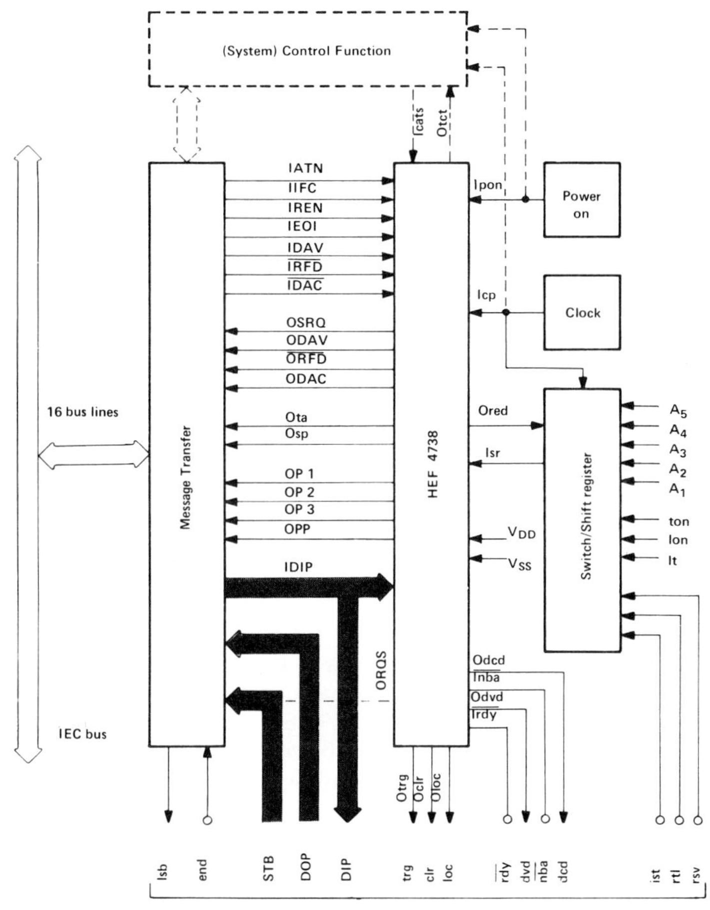

Fig. 5.4   HEF-4738 installed with interface (courtesy Grimberg)

trigger, device clear, remote/local, and service request are present. A 10 MHz single phase clock is used (see Fig. 5.7).

In a practical example, the 96LS488 was used for the design of a straightforward programmable power supply. The block diagram is reproduced in Fig. 5.8. The ASCII values from the data bus are decoded in the accessory logic, storing the bcd numbers and converting them to a binary format before passing on to a D to A converter. The converter's output drives the DC output amplifier, namely the variable power supply output itself. Manual or local

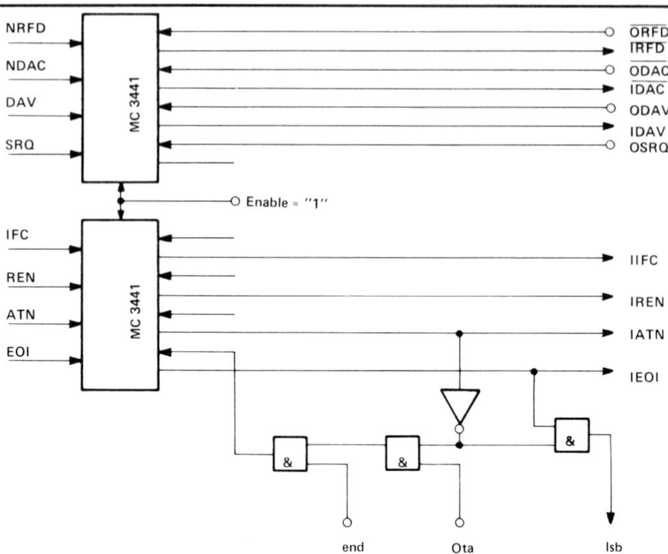

Fig. 5.5

voltage programming is possible via a thumbwheel logic control switch feeding the multiplexer. Overload detection is present which is directed to the appropriate terminals (RSV—request service) of the interface chip signalling a fault or error condition and actuating the SRQ. Remote reset is possible which allows the controller to clear the supply to zero by a single command and thus clear the overload. In this design example single byte addressing is used with talker/listener operation. As an addressed active listener (LACS) the instrument receives data on the bus and will recognise and store two ASCII coded decimal digits. The bus message delimiter is a CR character, signalling transfer of the numeric value down the chain to set the output voltage. When powered up the interface is self clearing and defaults to the local or manual condition. Front panel indicators signal its control condition—overload, remote or addressed, and the 'local' button which takes the chip RTL (return to local) line to ground 'true', asserts local operation for the instrument, disengaging it from bus control.

PERIPHERALS

Strictly speaking peripherals are devices which relate to the computer. Traditionally they rely on specialised computer type interfaces

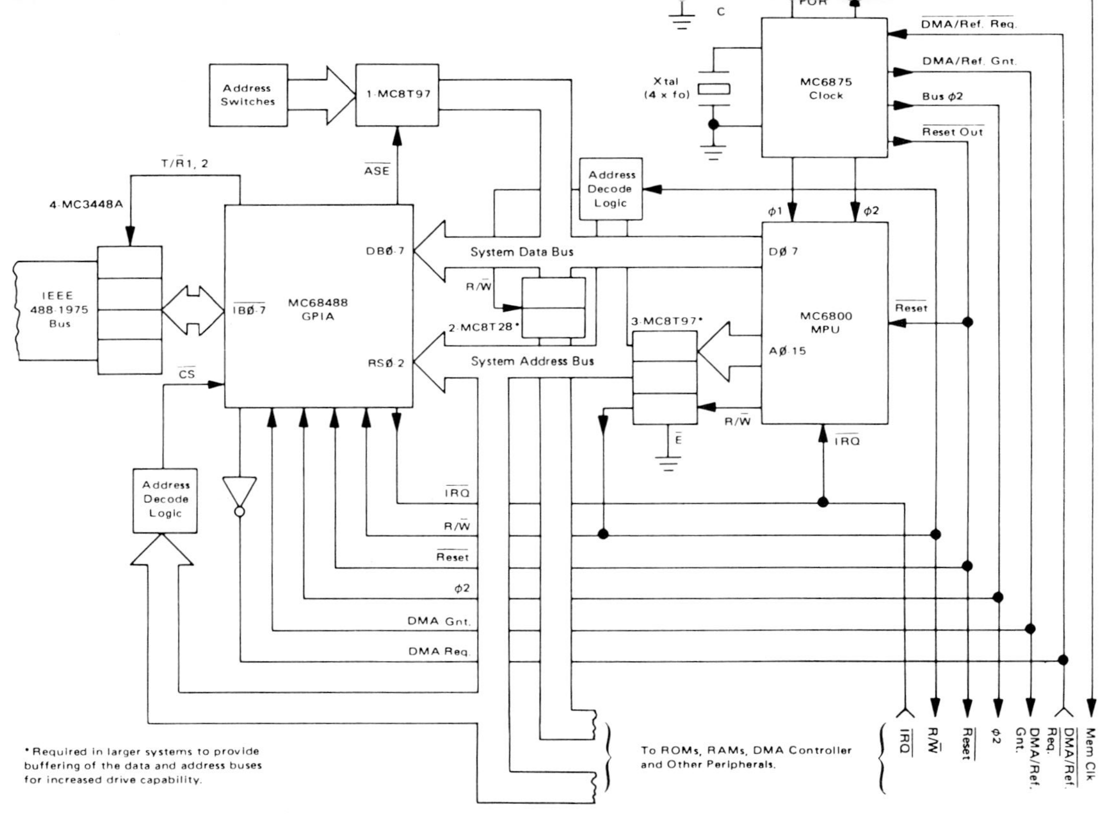

Fig. 5.6   A microprocessor based integrated circuit interface (courtesy Motorola)

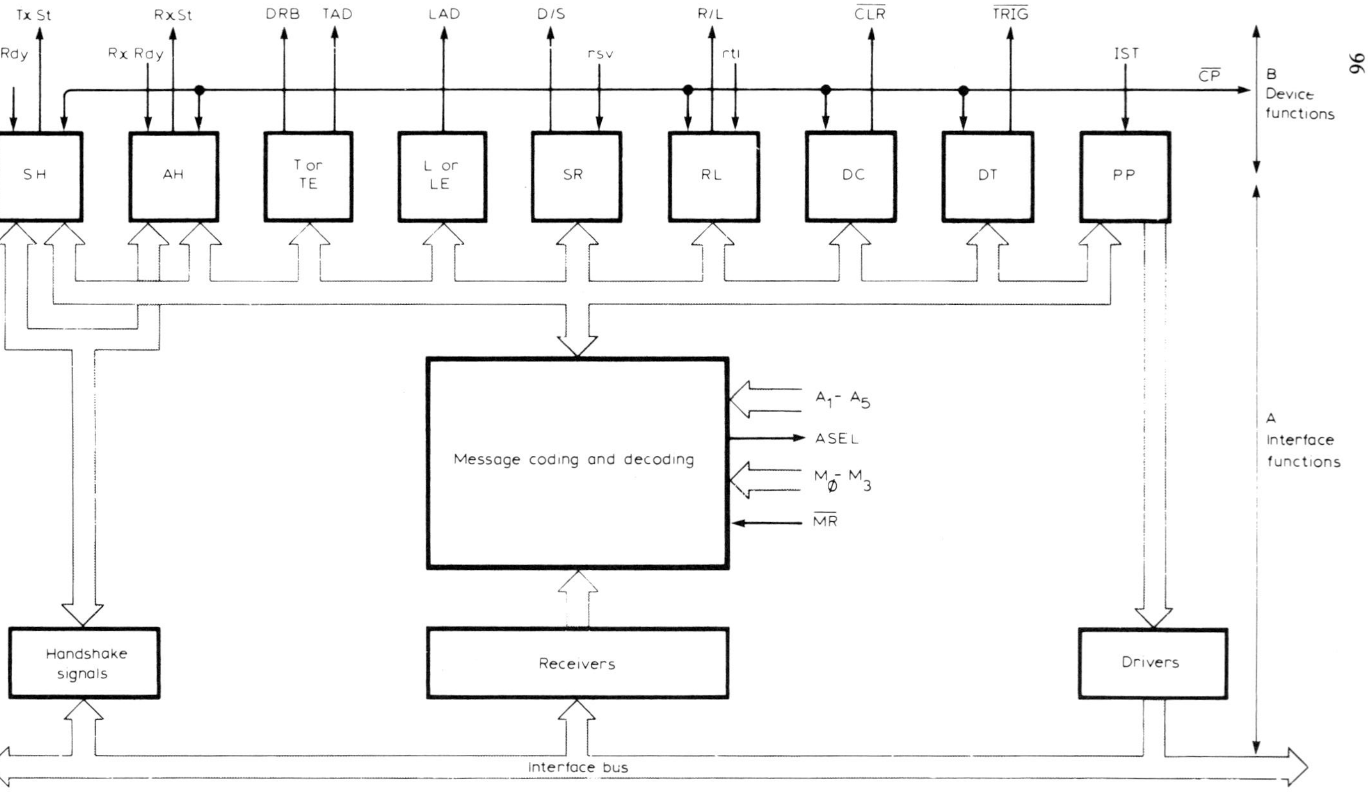

Fig. 5.7 Integrated interface chip, Fairchild 96LS488 functional block diagram

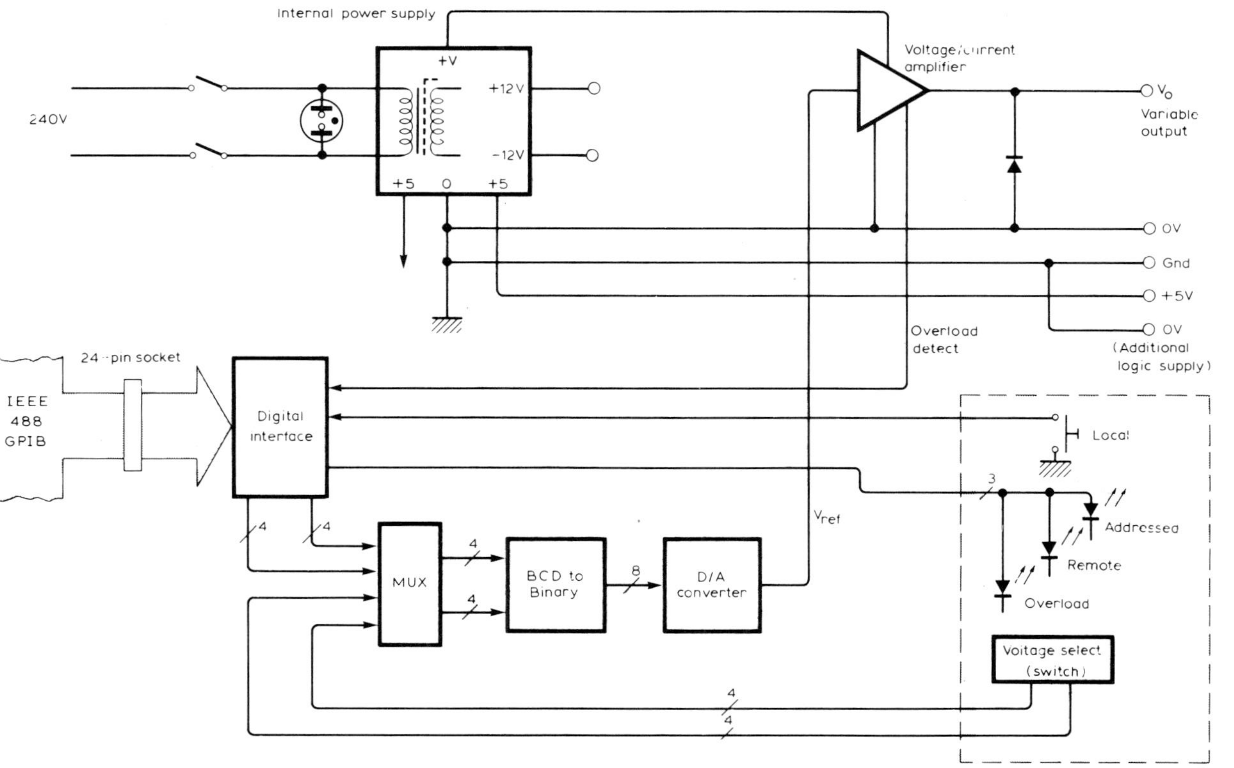

Fig. 5.8 Programmable power supply block diagram using integrated chip (courtesy Wireless World)

for interconnection and communication. However, dissemination of the bus is proceeding at such a rate that many bus interfaced peripherals are now becoming available. As with instrumentation, bus designed peripherals may be readily joined to the system and the tasks of data storage and documentation for the test engineer are in consequence generally eased.

The competitive nature of the computer market, particularly with respect to peripherals, has resulted in keen pricing for many of these devices. The peripheral designers are also coming up with new ways of handling and processing information; for example many inexpensive dot matrix printers, both thermal and impact, are now available with quite useful graphic facilities. In many cases entire screen displays may be dumped onto paper with little or no extra programming. This latter aspect is a key factor, since the alternative graphics solution of a high performance precision vector plotter is not only expensive as hardware, but also requires appropriate programming to produce the data in the required form. The cost saving afforded by the 'dump screen' of the cheaper printers is an important factor. Conversely the vector plotters are unrivalled where high-quality graphs suitable for publication are required, and in their current 'intelligent' forms, they can also annotate their graphs in a variety of alphanumeric styles. In a similar manner the dot matrix print quality of the cheaper printers may be upgraded to better quality print by substituting a model from the range of fast spinwheel or daisy wheel printhead machines available.

Mass storage

The specific controller chosen for a system may have no permanent inbuilt data or program storage, or those which are provided are of limited use, perhaps in terms of speed or capacity. In the latter category fall the slow and inexpensive audio cassette based data stores of 59 to 100K byte capacity. Reading or writing of longer programs via such stores can take 10 minutes or more, but the more advanced controllers may include a precision cartridge tape storage of higher performance which differentiates them from the humbler audio or mini cassette type. The better drives are more reliable with lower error rates and adequately fast access times. For example, the drive fitted to the HP85 is fairly typical, and offers a search speed of 8K byte/s, a transfer rate of 650K byte/s with a 210K byte total data capacity. Sensible file organisation on the cartridge provides a typical program access time of under 10 s. Such a store is suitable for fairly simple programs which are not accessed too frequently—once or twice a day perhaps. It also has uses for long-term storage and is convenient for program exchanges.

However, where data needs to be rapidly and frequently accessed, a disc type store is essential. A bewildering variety exists from the ubiquitous $5\frac{1}{4}$ in mini floppy to the 8 in floppy and the hard disc Winchester stores. The biggest units offer reliable performance in capacities of 2 to 10M byte, and may be used in combination to even greater capacities.

Where more complex programs are involved, particularly those involving the fast storage of a large data field, disc is essential; for example, in a production test arrangement where filing and storage of data over considerable periods is required, even 2M bytes of store can be exploited surprisingly quickly. Likewise, inventories and similar bulky data files need disc storage to take advantage of the rapid access available within the data base.

Looking at performances, the comparatively inexpensive $5\frac{1}{4}$ in mini floppy disc typically offer a 150 to 300K byte capacity, with a 10 to 20K byte/s transfer rate and a typical access time of 0.3 s or less. Such disc drives are now found on a number of controller computers and the storage may usually be extended by adding further external disc drives. Eight-inch floppy discs lead towards the Winchester, offering over 1M byte capacity per disc with 25K byte/s transfer rates, and once again these may be 'stacked'. Hewlett-Packard are the main producers of bus compatible disc stores, but other manufacturers are emerging in a field traditionally dominated by special computer dedicated interfaces.

A high performance hard disc 'Winchester' unit can provide typically a 20M byte capacity with transfer rates approaching 1M byte/s and access times of around 0.04 s. In terms of the cost per stored byte, the user by no means pays excessively for this performance compared with the humbler systems; in fact, the cost per byte is generally lower than for the $5\frac{1}{4}$ in floppy. With disc storage units the programming and formatting can be quite complicated, and for some of the less expensive controllers this can add considerably to the software cost. Often a disc operating system (DOS), either as software or an additional ROM, forms an essential part of the arrangement, and further machine memory (RAM) is usually required to service these disc operating routines. Here, as in all cases involving software, the buyer must assess the ease of use and flexibility of the storage system which may be required. In some cases this consideration will extend directly to the host computer, since it is often the latter's ability to handle data logically and efficiently which determines the software simplicity of the mass storage installation. A more costly disc store might repay its expense many times over in ease and speed of retrieval of data files and in the programmed quality of the organisation of those files.

Where the purchase of standard software is relevant to the buyer's proposed application, the choice of storage and controller type should reflect compatibility not only with disc size but also with the required software and it is therefore vital that the requirements of a bus orientated system are thoroughly researched before purchase. The key here is a thorough system analysis whereby a complete system—both the overall test or control arrangement and the details of the computer and its peripherals and interfaces (hardware and software)—are minutely examined and organised on paper.

Hard copy: printers, plotters

Documentation of the operation and results generated by an automated or semi-automated system is a valuable facility. While it is true that the data may be stored during operation for plotting or printing at a later stage, it is usually worth adding a hard copy peripheral to the installation for continuous readout of past data.

A vast range of printers is now available and while the majority have so far come equipped with RS232 teletype compatible interfaces, bus compatible versions are rapidly emerging. The commonest printer types use an impact dot matrix for character generation, with the least expensive versions employing a low resolution 5×7 field. The resolution limits character quality and low grade or omitted descenders and other related imperfections are present. They can be fast, delivering up to 250 characters per second, but note should be taken of time lost for carriage return. Bi-directional machines dispense with the 'carriage return' by storing a line ahead and printing it backwards as the matrix head sweeps back to the start position. Other features to note with all printers are the specification, expense and availability of the paper they use; can it be obtained in bulk rolls to reduce the frequency of reloading the printer and does the printer need an accessory device to feed it paper, etc.?

Dot matrix printers can offer finer matrices, of up to 9×7 dots on a half space overlap font, and true descenders are possible; the resolution providing much better letter quality, though still of recognisably dot matrix origination. Where fine resolution matrices are concerned, microprocessor control of character generation rather than simple ASCII letter translation allows great versatility of character font, as well as the incorporation of characters specific to national usage. Furthermore, microprocessor control has allowed the incorporation of graphics facilities which in many cases enable the printer to supplant the role of a true graphics plotter. Often the interfacing is so straightforward that the entire alphanumerics and graphics content of a computer display may be 'dumped' on the printer paper. Matrices of up to 14×15 have been used, and microprocessor control removes the need to specify the first or horizontal number component; hence the terms $N \times 9$ or $N \times 12$ where N is a micro-derived variable.

Perhaps less popular matrix printers include the electrosensitive paper types, where an aluminised silver paper is written by electric current discharge from the print head. Easier to read thermal printers use temperature sensitive paper, usually blue or more recently with a black impression. These are fast and also relatively quiet which may be an important requirement in some applications, but the thermal print paper is a little smudgy in quality, and has a limited life before the print gradually fades; a slight deterioration is noticeable after a few months. Cool storage out of the light will help but for long-term record keeping this could be a problem.

Where industrial applications are concerned, it is also worth verifying that a printer is capable of scientific notation such an upper case for exponents. Many of the less expensive printers are inadequate in this respect. Two classes of graphics printer exist, namely those which use special characters or character elements to produce low resolution graphics, and those with full processor dot control which can give virtually continuous high resolution graphic plots.

If high-quality documentation is required, then a better-quality printer is essential. Costing two to three times the price of a typical matrix printer, these 'daisy' or 'spinwheel' printers cannot offer the high resolution graphics facility and are restricted to the character set on the usually interchangeable print head wheel. In quality the print is closest to an electric typewriter, though not quite IBM golfball standard. Speeds are also lower than matrix at typically 40 characters per second or less.

Finally, the hard copy group comprises the true plotters. These are bus interfaced flat-bed units resembling the traditional XY analogue plotter. The less expensive designs are often based on a traditional analogue mechanism, together with appropriate adaptors for conversion to the digital data code sent on the bus. A3 paper size is common, though A4 is often more convenient in terms of both paper size and the bench space occupied. It is interesting that the least expensive digital plotters cost little more than their analogue partner counterparts and can still offer a wide range of facilities. The best known is probably the Japanese Watanabe DIGI-PLOT WX4671, an A3 machine which can be bus configured and which offers internal programming for chart axes, several line types plus alphanumeric

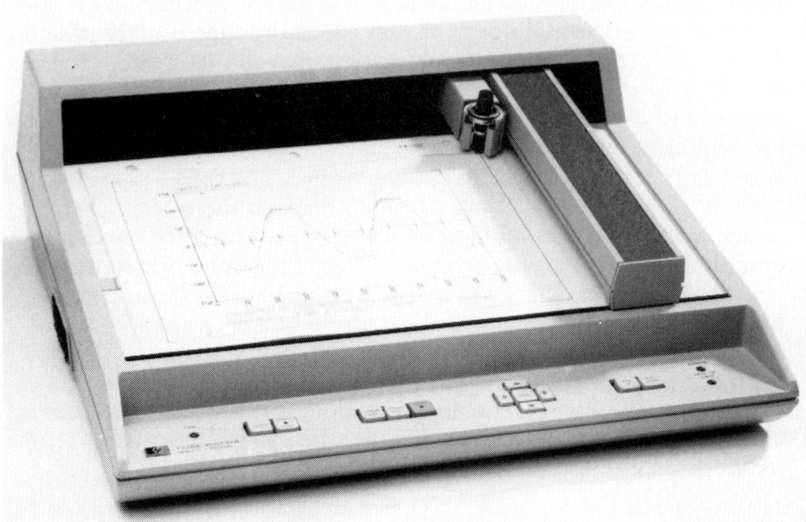

Fig. 5.9   GPIB microstep controlled vector plotter, HP-7225A (courtesy Hewlett-Packard)

annotation in various sizes and slants amongst its many facilities. The HP7470A, a compact A4 two-colour machine also appears in this category. Using fibre-tip pens these plotters offer clean lines of near draughtsman quality, exhibiting fine accuracy and repeatability.

The classic moderate cost digital A4 plotter is Hewlett-Packard's HP7225. Using 'HPGL', the graphics orientated HP language, it offers a versatile performance of excellent accuracy. Such machines may also be operated in reverse as digitisers where the pen can be manually positioned over the required points on a specified drawing and the data point position encoded and fed back to the computer. The data can then be processed, e.g., an unspecified graph could be synthesised and its mathematical equation determined. Alternatively the data could be processed to replot a reduced scale version, or a magnified section (Fig. 5.9).

Multicolour plotters are also available. A programmed command instructs the moving head to retrieve up to eight different colour pens from a store. Hewlett-Packard, Bryans Southerns and Philips all produce models of this type.

It has been mentioned that alphanumerics may be plotted, a very useful feature for scales and title labels. However, if used as a 'printer' (which is possible with most models), the print speed would be very low and in the long term would result in unnecessary wear.

Specialised units

The general range of industrial test instrumentation is undoubtedly well known to the reader, with a high percentage of units now provided with bus interfacing. However, certain product categories receive rather less attention, possibly because they are lacking in glamour, which is unfortunate as they can represent vital components in an automatic test system.

A key instrument is the programmable switch-box, also known by other names, such as 'scanner'. Its function is to make the necessary electrical interconnections to units in the system, both the DUT and test equipment, according to the requirements of the operating program. Good examples of the genre are modular, so that module combinations appropriate to the type of signal being handled may be selected. For example, a 20 A relay switch suitable for linking high current loads to a power amplifier would not be applicable to low level millivolt signal switching at the same amplifier's input terminal. Likewise where small dc voltages are concerned low thermal contacts are required, while in the case of high frequency signals, low capacitance switches of good voltage standing wave ratio are essential. Modular switch-boxes are often sufficiently versatile to allow for custom selection or modification of the switch type, and in addition they may possess optional plug-ins capable of limited measurement of raw signals. Digital voltmeter plug-ins are also common, allowing digitally converted data to be placed on the bus; those in stripped-down form may be an array of A to D convertors. Where many signal lines are to be monitored, these scanner units can have a number of convertor sections installed, each individually monitoring the sensor lines, for example, as in process control. When bus interfaces were fairly costly, certain manufacturers designed low cost instrument ranges with an inexpensive simplified interface, usually a BCD variant as an interim solution. Groups of these related instruments could then be bus interfaced via a single common bus translator unit, thus sharing the interface cost among several devices. The Fluke range is a good example of this type, and other producers include Keithly, Farnell and Tektronix, the latter's programmable TM500 system falling more or less into this category (Fig. 3.9).

EXTENDERS

With a 20 m total cable limit on the bus, computer control over longer distances requires the use of an extender. It is perfectly feasible to remotely control a test system via a telephone line by using suitable extenders and telephone coupling modems. The RS232 interface is often used for long wire interconnections, but the best speeds are achieved by more advanced fibre optic link extenders such as the HP1205A which can offer 20K byte/s data rates up to 100 m. The HP37201A can operate over simple twisted-pair wire cables up to 1 km long at up to 20K bits/s (8 bits to a byte).

FUTURE DEVELOPMENT

The field of voice interaction is developing rapidly in computing with the most common facility comprising inexpensive add-on boards for many computer controllers to provide a speech output. Properly organised, such a facility would eliminate the need for an operator to look out for prompts on an alphanumeric display: in fact, these could be eliminated altogether. For general purpose applications, however, the vocabulary of the present units is small, a few hundred words, but in the case of the narrow requirements of a test arrangement this is not a problem. Voice input is much harder for the computer; and requires voice pattern recognition, but again the vocabulary required for controller-operator interaction is small enough to permit important developments in this field in the near future. If quick decisions and reactions are involved, or where the systems operator cannot have immediate access to the set-up or a keyboard, voice I/O facilities could prove an important advantage and be incorporated in a bus interfaced peripheral to be added to existing systems. Easily under-estimated but nonetheless an important aspect of voice I/O is its humanising character helping to make computer systems more friendly to non-technical users.

6

Programming hangups, bus analysers and extenders

INTRODUCTION

Enthusiastic claims for the bus may have given rise to the impression that bus system planning is foolproof. While it is undoubtedly true that the GPIB is superior to the many non-uniform instrument control and data interfaces previously in use, and is a high performance link in its own right, the system as a whole is not entirely free of problems. The gradual evolution from the first 1975 IEEE publication is partly responsible, as is incomplete understanding on the part of some instrument and interface designers of what is admittedly a complex digital interface. The solution of some of these problems involves bus analysers which will also be examined. Finally, the design and use of bus extenders will be covered, these increasing the scope and power of the GPIB.

PROGRAMMING HANGUPS

Probably the largest number of programming hangups result from the historic absence of a software standard. Recently introduced documents on the subject are framed as recommended practice rather than as a standard, though 625-2 and IEEE 728 will undoubtedly be a great help in the future if their recommendations are followed. In Chapter 1, some bus operation anomalies were mentioned, and the CBM Pet series of controllers and their lack of complete bus implementation has been referred to in other chapters.

Simple hangups can occur as a result of incompatible message delimiters between devices, and the IEC625-2 suggests that to aid backward compatibility new devices should have as much interpretation flexibility as possible. In listen mode it is suggested that devices be forgiving in their acceptance of data, i.e., should not only accept data which is in the exact defined formats but also messages that may carry minor variations in format structure. Some of these might be due to inadvertent human error—extra or missed spaces, for example, or to a limited output formatting capability, the latter resulting from cost or performance restraints.

Of the eight data lines, seven are used for ASCII/ISO character code transmission while the eighth is set aside as a parity bit. Recent devices seem to agree on the use of a 'low' parity bit, while earlier controllers generally followed a 'high' convention.

In an effort to improve the compatibility of number formats, new controllers are becoming more flexible. The TEK 4041 and HP9845, for example, offer multiple data acceptance and storage formats. 'Integer' mode permits compact storage of data of 16 bits or less, such as 12-bit A to D convertor outputs. 'Short floating point' gives the convenience of decimal point arithmetic and speed when seven significant digits are enough and, finally, 'long floating point' provides 15 digit accuracy—sufficient for the output of a 10-digit counter or frequency meter, though at a cost of four times the memory space of the integer alternative.

In the language of IEC 625-2 (and the ISO/ANSI number representations) numbers having a zero value and a negative sign should be accepted (NR1–NR3), though this is normally ruled out. Although NR3 representation should be signed, the lack of sign should not bar acceptance by the listening device. When a number is received which is larger or of greater precision than the listener can handle the latter should 'round off' the value rather than truncate or otherwise corrupt it.

While upper case capital letters are specified for HR (header fields) it is helpful if the listener will accept lower case as equivalent; this is particularly useful where controllers are involved which generally have an upper and lower case facility. Another recommendation states that a listener should not hold its acceptor function in ACDS using the NDAC assert and hold. When bus transfers need to be suspended by a listener it should assert and hold the appropriate line, namely NRFD. SRQ is classed as an asynchronous event and thus, if possible, should not be used or understood as an immediate interrupt. Where a device is designed to require fast controller service on SRQ assertion this should be pointed out clearly in the device documentation.

Other problems which can arise with older instruments include their measurement data, which may need to be in special form such as a HEX code digital string. A controller which can easily handle the various number forms is clearly an advantage.

Delimiters or end of message terminators are also a source of trouble and a controller with the ability to select end of message terminators, e.g., CR or LF, is a decided advantage. On the listener side these character variants should be recognised in addition to EOI and its alternatives.

Interrupt handling is important, particularly where a high priority process or data transfer is under way. The ability to define levels of interrupt priority and to make the system fail-safe on interrupt is valuable.

After drafting the 1978 revision to the 1975 IEEE-488 standard an oversight in the standard was discovered which relates to certain TCS (take control synchronously) conditions whereby the DAB (data byte) could be misinterpreted as an improper message. It may be corrected by adding a CSHS (Controller Standby Hold State) for the C (Controller) function to delay ATN assertion, thus circumventing the possible simultaneous assertion of DAV and ATN read by an idle device.

Where block data is used, mainly for extended length messages, problems may occur concerning buffer size and availability, and sometimes a listening device will prove incapable of accepting long records.

Some instruments may lack a complete implementation of the bus and thus cause hangups due to the inability of the controller to adequately make its commands understood by the listening instrument. Such problems can occur with older converted arrangements, such as a complex analyser adapted to the bus via an RS232 port of inferior program level. These combinations often require rather cryptic command codes with binary or similar data formats and can be very costly in software time. Prospects for bus adapting earlier generation digital instruments must be viewed with great caution.

While simple bus systems can be up and running quickly, the more complex arrangements involving timing and synchronisation can cause problems. Their development may make a bus analyser essential to investigate hangups involving system time delays due to bus subroutines which are normally neither 'visible' to the user nor are they usually of any great interest.

When a bus operated system has been running for some time, possibly years, bugs or hangups may appear. Hardware faults, which are not obvious, may also appear on the interface and can be difficult to troubleshoot. Whatever the source of the bug, which may simply be the failure of the programmer or operator to properly appreciate the relationship between a command and the result of that command in the context of a particular instrument, a bus analyser may be helpful for troubleshooting.

BUS ANALYSERS

Bus analysers come in a wide variety of forms to help evaluate bus interfaces in specific instruments and to debug system faults. When trouble shooting at the interface level it should be noted that quite simple BASIC controller level commands can result in a burst of interface commands and that the analyser must be large enough in step memory size to cope with a realistic number of transmission messages. While an engineer may be aware of the bus level commands and their standard meanings he may still be confused by the strange effects resulting with some instruments when fed standard commands. In one example, a device interprets a parallel poll as an error and generates an SRQ, this can cause an immediate hangup if the controller transmits a parallel poll message during system initialisation, since the origin of the offending SRQ is not then accessible to the controller.

Intelligent instruments which operate perfectly along on the bus can nonetheless inexplicably hangup the bus. For example, many microprocessor instruments run a self-test routine on power-up without due consideration to the effects of their spurious outputs on other devices already powered. The bus can be inexplicably locked by the random combinations of message data so that the offending device is hard to trace.

While a system controller can be used to trouble-shoot the bus, helped by a bus printer monitoring message traffic, the printer artificially slows bus operations and additionally the high data volume from a controller can hide the fine detail of bus operations from the trouble shooter. Dedicated devices such as the Tektronix DAS9100, a digital pattern generator, can be very helpful though at a price. On this instrument the bus lines may be toggled to verify correct operation, a feature also of some far less expensive devices, though the latter cannot match the combination of bus level and high level controller programming available with the more sophisticated designs.

It may be necessary to sequentially remove instruments physically from a bus system to determine which one causes the hangup. Some of the more subtle problems can arise from pulse ringing on the bus lines or when, as sometimes occurs, a device is sensitive to pulse edges rather than the properly established logic levels.

Analysers range from Systron Donner's little status line indicator PIN 073663 which provides test points for DIO_{1-8} and for eight more control lines, REN, ATN, IFC, SRQ, NDAC, NRFD, DAV, EOI. Eight LEDS additionally monitor the logic state on these lines.

Ziatech (USA) have produced the ZT488, another low-cost unit, again employing rows of LED indicators to monitor bus line status. Capable of being classed as a bus analyser rather than a test/monitor fixture, as in the case of the Systron Donner, it can emulate a bus device in monitor role or act as a manual system controller. Switches on the panel allow bus control and manual entry of data values. Two versions are produced, one for a 5 V logic power supply and one for US 115 V mains, the latter at higher cost.

Battery powered at twice the price of the Ziatech, Racal-Dana offers the 488, which does not disturb bus operation while monitoring. Virtually a hand-held unit, it can store sequences of up to forty discrete bus level transactions. These are displayed in the hexadecimal notation on a liquid crystal display which includes information on the memory location, the data and the following lines: ATN, SRQ, EOI and NDAC. Panel switches allow manual setting of ATN, SRQ, EOI and of the data line triggers through DOI_{1-8}. The unit is capable of capturing data before and after the trigger condition.

It can be argued that due to the high density of bus level transmissions greater step storage is necessary. ICS Electronics 4810 has memory sufficient for 100 steps. At a further two times price increase over the Racal unit, the ICS4810 can act as a bus controller, transmitting its entire memory of transactions if preprogrammed or entered. A loop is incorporated to allow a message stored in memory to be repeated and unused memory sections may be skipped. Its versatility extends to choices of data rate from single step manual mode, 500K byte/s, 2M bytes/s or variable under the control of an external clock at up to 4 MHz. Display flexibility includes hexadecimal data line LED read out, decimal memory location, and individual indicators for the control and status lines (Fig. 6.1).

A related instrument is also available from Hewlett-Packard, the 59401A. Though more costly still, the step memory is relatively small at 32 bus characters. Its particular details include operating speeds of one manual step at a time, two steps per second, normal bus speed or under control of an external clock up to 10 MHz. With a compare mode operating at bus speeds, bus traffic may be automatically stopped at a preselected character. An accompanying trigger pulse is provided which can prove invaluable for the analysis of bus transient or timing problems. Another feature is the data display in Octal and ASCII.

Still on an increasing price spiral a considerable advance in performance is provided by the 488 bus analyser made in the USA by Interface Technology. Here the step or transaction unit memory is expanded to 511 and will store at rates of up to 250K byte/s. It is suitable both for bus trouble shooting and for assessing individual device compliance with the standard. Data is displayed in hex and bus

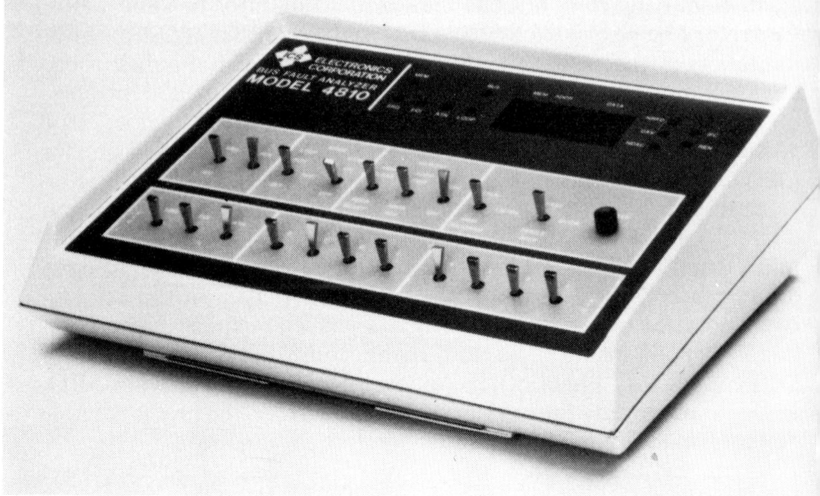

Fig. 6.1 Compact bus analyser, ICS-4810

mnemonics, the usual indicators monitor control and status lines and the bus addresses are given in decimal. Operating as a programmable bus controller it can run up to 255 bus message sequences, and 32K bytes of **EPROM** is provided to store up to 100 programs. Programs may be written in machine code or high level language and edited using the front panel keyboard. Fault detection modes seek out hardware errors such as a failure in handshake or static condition, data errors including comparison failure, early or missing termination and status errors such as incorrect byte transmitted by a device.

Above this level one enters the realm of true high performance logic analysers in whose domains the GPIB is just another logic data/control bus.

Some simple logic analysers are available equipped for bus duty and offer an alternative view of bus level transactions. Hewlett-Packard's model 1602A fitted with the 10051A GPIB 'probe' can decode its LED readouts into mixed formats for bus use, e.g., binary for the control and status lines, and hex for the data group (Fig. 6.2). More advanced analysers are produced by HP, Tektronix, Dolch Logic Instruments and Gould-Advance. The latter company's Biomation K100-D analyser offers either asynchronous or synchronous operation together with separate connections to allow monitoring of up to eight signals outside the bus. The display

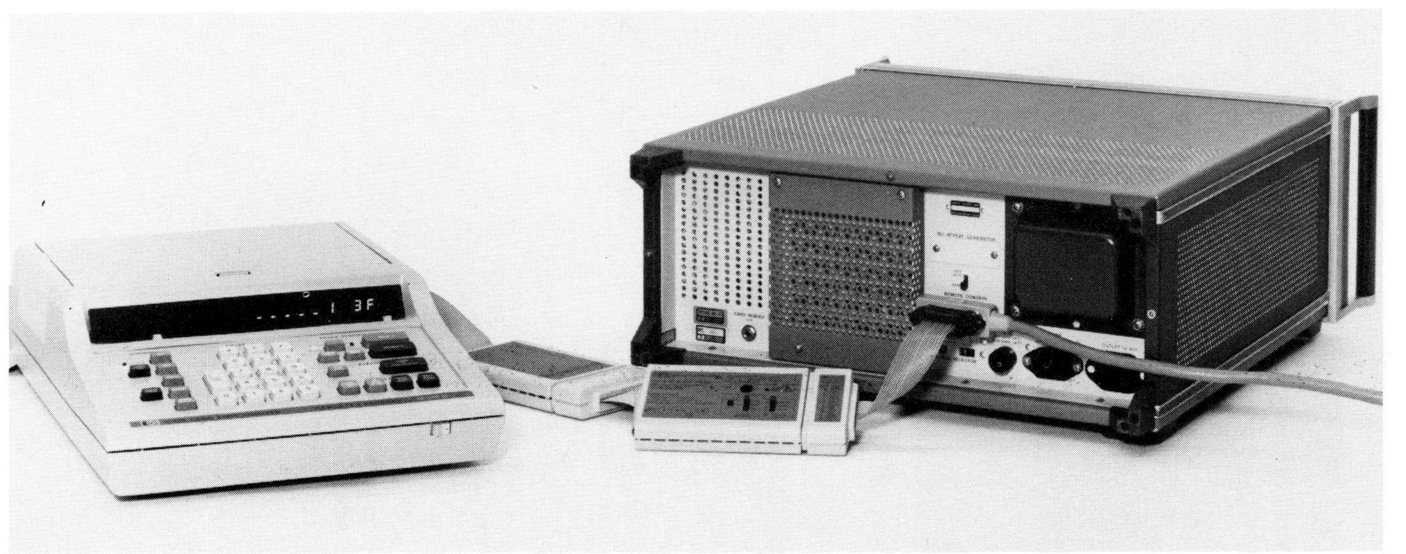

Fig. 6.2   HP-1602A

```
DATA A  SPCL       CLOCK  10 nSEC          DELAY    500 CLOCKS
                   6543210   F E D      C B A 9 8
          C  181      J      0 1 0      0 0 0 1 0
             182      :      0 1 0      0 0 1 0 0
             183      B      0 1 1      1 1 1 0 0
             184  1111100    0 1 0      0 0 0 1 0
             185      D      0 1 0      0 1 0 0 0
             186      <      0 1 0      0 0 0 1 0
             187      @      0 1 0      0 0 0 1 0
             188     STX     0 0 1      1 1 1 0 0
             189      <      0 1 0      0 0 0 1 0
             190     DLE     0 1 1      1 1 1 0 0
             191     DLE     0 0 0      1 0 0 0 0
             192     DLE     0 0 0      1 0 0 0 0
             193      B      0 0 0      1 0 0 0 0
             194      B      0 1 0      0 0 0 1 0
             195      B      0 1 0      0 0 0 1 0
             196      <      0 1 0      0 0 0 1 0
             197      B      0 1 0      0 0 0 1 0
             198      $      0 1 0      0 0 0 1 0
             199     CAN     0 0 1      0 0 1 0 0
             200      B      0 0 0      1 1 0 0 0

     RDY    T: 500    C( 181)   R( 258)   P-C =   +77   0.77-5
```

Fig. 6.3   Biomation KD100D analyser display of bus messages (courtesy Gould Advance)

flexibility encompasses waveform, binary, octal, hexadecimal and ASCII format of bus activity. In Fig. 6.3 the Biomation display shows the management and handshake signals (channels F-8) in binary while the data channels (6—0) are in ASCII, e.g., line 183. Data sequences not corresponding to an ASCII character are automatically shown in binary; for example, in line 184. In its analysis of events and signal timing it can work to a 10 ns resolution and at synchronous recording rates of up to 10 MHz.

The Dolch LAM3250 and LAM4850A units differ in that both synchronous and asynchronous monitoring is simultaneously permissible via split memories.

The more costly HP1610B and 1615A (plus 10066A probe) analysers are highly sophisticated, offering easily formatted displays, CRT menu style operation and multilevel keyboard programming, although these powerful instruments cost more than many high performance bus controllers.

Two quality analyser systems are offered by Tektronix, one based on the 7000 series oscilloscope main-frame and comprising the combination of DF2 display formatter and 7DO1 logic analyser plugins (Fig. 6.4). The mnemonic translation of bus codes is just one of the useful features of the system. A more costly and more recent stand along digital analyser from Tektronix is the DAS9100 (Fig. 6.5) which combines logic analysis with pattern recognition, mass storage, and communication interfaces, including GPIB. A modular based system, it is intrinsically very powerful with facilities for up to 104 channels at

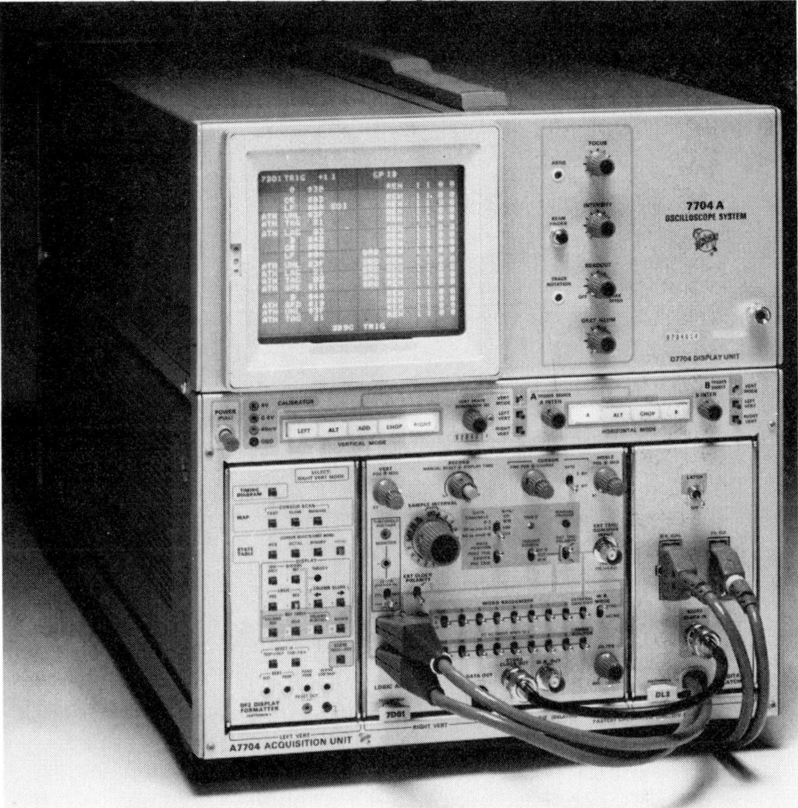

Fig. 6.4   Analyser display, Tektronix DF2 (courtesy Tektronix)

up to 330 MHz sample rates and it is itself a GPIB device as well as a
bus analyser when appropriately configured. The 23cm raster scan
display is complemented by a mass storage cartridge. A 512-word
memory is available: acquisition may be synchronous and/or asynchronous and the keyboard/menu system is incorporated for rapid
selection of the required operating modes. Full message and program
editing is possible together with enhancements such as magnification
of the timing diagram for increased resolution.

EXTENDERS

The GPIB is intended for running small groups of controlled test
systems with a total cable length of 20 m, and a 2 m maximum

Fig. 6.5   The DAS 9100 high performance logic analyser (courtesy Tektronix)

between two adjacent devices or interfaces. This rule can be broken but only at the expense of potential system reliability problems which would be very difficult to trace and solve.

There are situations where it might prove useful to operate a remote bus installation, possibly including a controller, from a local site; the separation between the two may be anything from 5 m to an indefinite distance, e.g., accessed via a public telephone system. Various solutions present themselves. The RS232 is an existing bus suitable for much longer cable runs than GPIB and many controllers already have it as an optional or standard facility. A telephone modem can also be used with the RS232. The main objection is that the complexity of GPIB transactions requires that the RS232 data be specially programmed to handle it, and it is difficult, if not impracticable, to fully implement the bus hardware. What is required is a fully coded single channel serial link which appears virtually transparent to the bus devices on each side communicating through the extender.

Early efforts in this area left some major gaps, for example, the pass control function was not available and often the parallel poll could not be implemented. Though certain timing and speed restrictions are inevitable the sophistication of extenders such as the HP37203A and the ICS 4886 has solved these anomalies.

Extenders can help with certain significant GPIB constraints. There is no electrical isolation between devices and this can cause

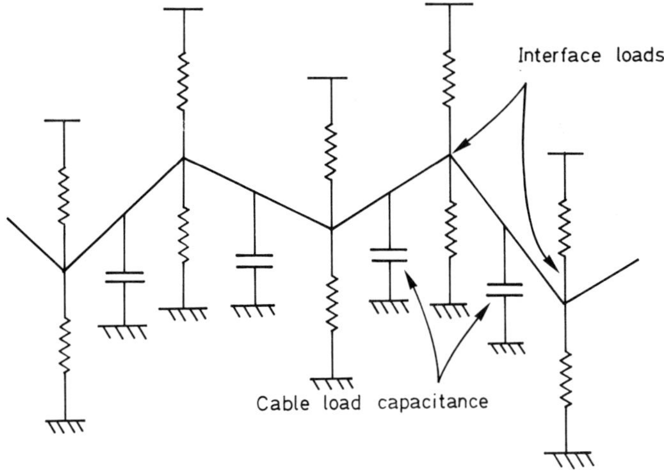

Fig. 6.6   Bus line chain

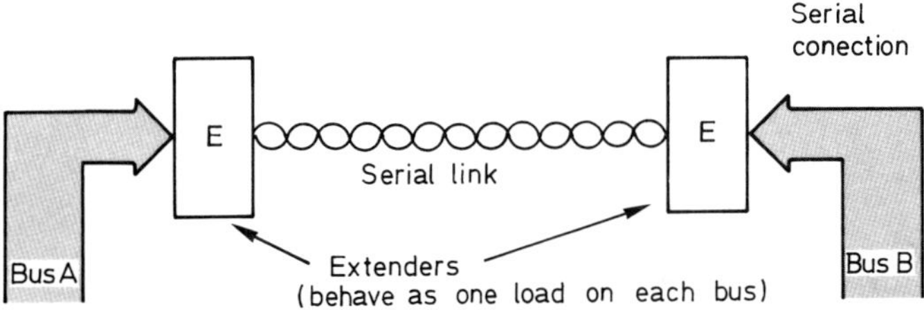

Fig. 6.7   Serial connection via extenders

problems in sensitive instruments and situations where interference and ground loops cause trouble. In the case of a particularly sensitive example of harmonic distortion analyser, threshold mid-band readings down to -104 dB at a particular input level were possible as a stand alone unit, but when linked to an active bus the threshold resolution was 10 dB poorer. An extender can offer electrical isolation.

Response times of 200 ns are normal on the bus and the typical cable length/interface termination/load generally gives a 1 μs time constant on the basis of 2 m cable, correctly loaded (Fig. 6.6).

Since an extender must use a serial data link the HPIB timing is inevitably affected. Twenty-five bits of serial code are needed for each bus byte. The timing also depends on the nature of the link (Fig. 6.7).

With the HP37203A several options are possible; dedicated coaxial

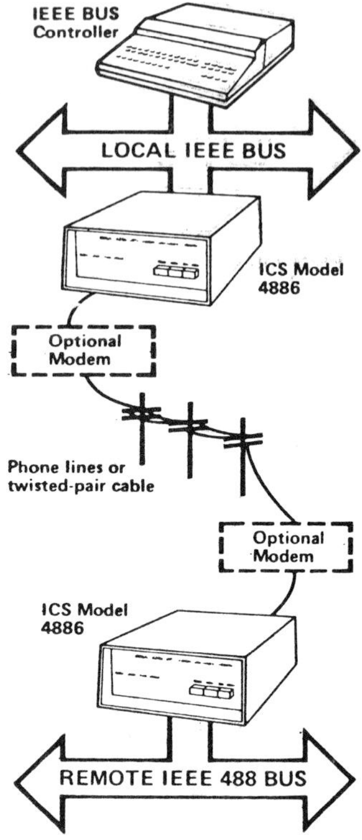

Fig. 6.8   Extender application (courtesy ICS)

cable, dedicated optical fibre or any other suitable medium. Working on transfer rates only, the fastest speed with a short coaxial length is 50K byte/s. Up to 250 m this will only reduce slightly, to 40K bytes/s, the maximum length for normal rate setting. With the rate progressively reduced to 1/16 of normal speed by 1 km of cable, the rate has fallen to 2.8K byte/s and problems of signal attenuation in the cable begin to dominate. Without repeaters, the use of longer cable runs is inadvisable and over 250 m the optical fibre option is superior. At 250 m the operating speed of coaxial and optical links are very similar but by 1 km the optical mode is nearly twice as fast.

ICS quote a range of up to 1,230 m using twisted-pair cabling operating in full duplex mode with simultaneous reception and transmission of data between the two extenders (Fig. 6.8). The data rate is much lower than the coaxial or optic link of Hewlett-Packard.

An incidental but possibly important feature of the extender is that

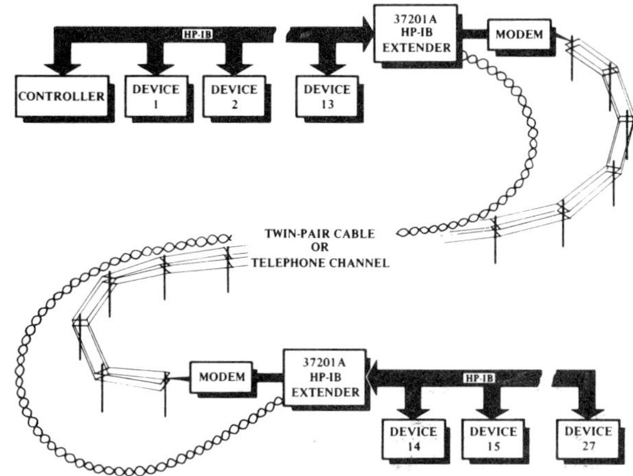

Fig. 6.9   Point-to-point connection using twin twisted-pair cable or full duplex modem link (courtesy Hewlett-Packard)

it overcomes the bus limitation of 14 devices plus controller since it can be used to link two bus systems, providing a total of 28 devices including controller; the extender pair themselves representing two devices (Fig. 6.9). Tandem and star multidrop arrangements can offer further system expansion.

Error checking

Transmission over public links can be unreliable due to dropout, transient noise, and poor signal quality. For reliable GPIB operation on such a link a failsafe and foolproof error correction system must be used, with a facility for system recovery if the link is broken entirely. In the case of the HP37203A, bus data is transmitted in frames or packets, each including a cyclic redundancy check code which is checked on receipt of the frame. Transmission errors are thus detected causing rejection of the frame. The operation system then automatically requests retransmission until uncorrupted frames are received.

In the case of the ICS 4886 an alternative system is used involving a combination of parity and check sum detection. The telephone network slows transmission to typically 800 bus bytes/s (20K bits/s) though this is quite sufficient for many applications. One application concerned a network of remote GPIB controlled and tested radio transmitters in outlying fringe reception areas of the country, the

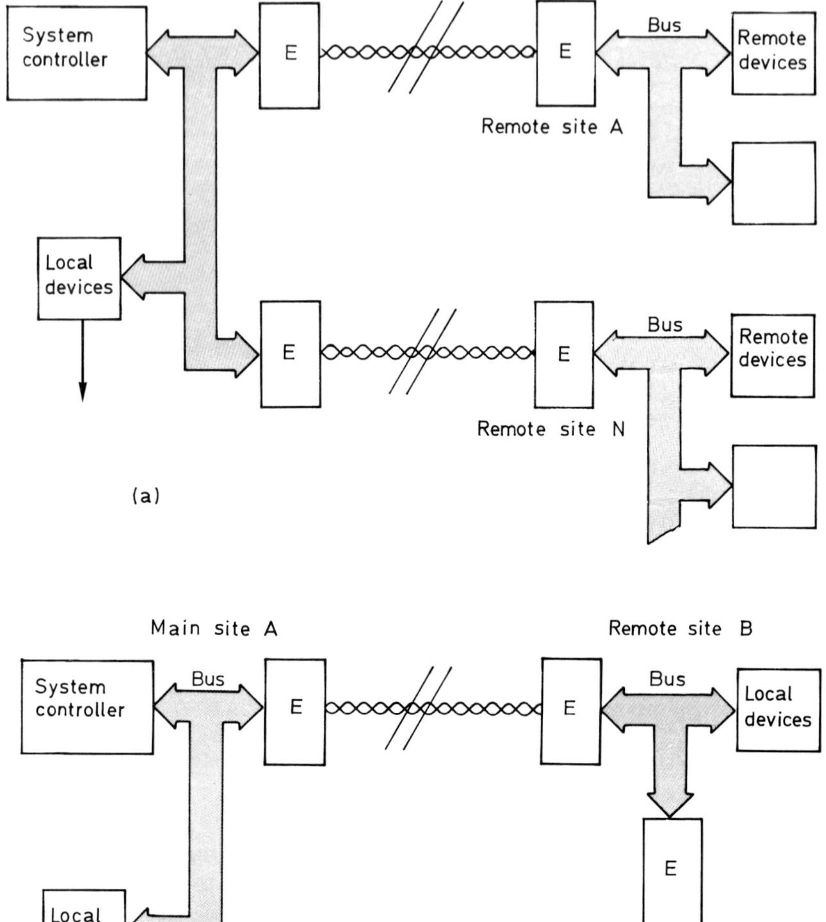

Fig. 6.10   (a) Star extension, (b) tandem extension

telephone link freeing these very small stations from the need for an on-site technician/operator. A test installation at one site could be lihked via the telephone to a duplicate installation at another site, both under central control for comparison, checking or synchronisation purposes. Once-a-day dialling to many remote sites for data collection is another good application. Some extenders may be addressed to control automatic dialling, automatic switch off and sequencing to the next site.

System configurations

Point to point transmission using single extender pairs has been covered (Figs. 6.10(a) and (b)). Star connection and tandem can provide multipoint systems.

Multidrop operation with the ICS 4886 is possible for up to 31 remote sites, with separate address numbers to identify each site.

Hardware

While the user does not need to know the internal workings of a bus extender it helps to explain the cost of these units by pointing out that if done properly, the entire bus is rebuilt and recoded digitally to achieve clean, long distance serial transmission. Since the bus can chatter a good deal faster than the link, the extender must store bus command sequences and queue them in order for proper sequencing. Considerable effort was expended before the programming of the extender hardware was sufficient for the task.

All that really matters to the user is that the extender pair integrates smoothly and transparently into the bus.

Bibliography

Amplicon Electronics Ltd., *The IEEE Interface Bus.*

van Andel, H., 'An automatic final test station for a $5\frac{1}{2}$ digit DDM'. Fluke paper presented at Testmex '80, London

Anundsen, R. L., *2nd Generation GPIB Equipment Offers Easy to Use Improvements.* Tektronix publication, Aug. 19 (1981)

Bruel & Kjaer, *Acoustical Measurements using the Digital Frequency Analyser Type 2131 with a Desk Top Calculator.* Bruel & Kjaer Application Note for bus control from HP 9825 controller

Colwill, P., 'Remote or local – a demarcation dispute'. Data Laboratories Ltd. paper presented at Testmex '80, London

Dance, M., 'Putting the GPIB in perspective', *Electronics Industry*, Feb. (1980) pp. 56–61

Datalab Instruments Ltd., *DL 2000 GPIB Operation.* Datalab Application Note 15

Datalab Instruments Ltd., *DL 420/20 GPIB Operation.* Datalab Application Note 7

Datalab Instruments Ltd., *CBM Pet IEEE 488 Interface Enhancements.* Datalab Application Note 13

Farnell Instruments Ltd., *An Introduction to the IEEE-588 Bus Standard*

Fisher, E. and Jensen, W., *Pet and the IEEE-488 Bus*, Osborne/McGraw-Hill, California

Genrad Instruments, *Using the Pet to Control the 1995.* Genrad Instruments Application Note and separate program listing

Grimberg, J. A. M., *IEC Bus Interface, Digital Instruments Course, Part 4.* Philips Test and Measurement Dept., Eindhoven

Harber, B. and Lytollis, B., 'Microprocessor simplifies automatic testing'. Marconi Ltd. paper presented at Testmex '81, London

Hewlett-Packard Co., *HPIB Programming Notes, (5952-9356)* Nov. (1980). For 8566A/8568A analysers with HP 9835/45 computers. Covers correct data transfers, measurements and harmonic distortion

Hewlett-Packard Co., *Audio and Transceiver Testing.* Application Note 300. A useful HP 85 based (BASIC) guide for auto-test systems using several programmable instruments.

Hewlett-Packard Co., *An Introduction to the 3582A Spectrum Analyser*

Hewlett-Packard Co., *85861A Software Pac Manual*

Hewlett-Packard Co., *HP 9826 BASIC Language System.* Hewlett-Packard Technical Data, May (1981)

Hewlett-Packard Co., *Hewlett-Packard Series 80 Hardware.* HP service document

Hewlett-Packard Co., *HP 85 I/O Programming Guide*

ICS Electronics Ltd., *Programming Hints for Pet and ICS Bus couplers.* Application Bulletin 48-7.

Loughry, D., 'ANSI/IEEE Standard 488 and HPIB', *Hewlett-Packard Journal*, Dec. (1979)

Marconi Instruments Ltd., The GPIB Manual.

Philips Ltd, *Instrumentation System Support ISS1*, Philips Application Note for CBM 2001-8, -16, -32, 3016 and 3032

Tektronix (UK) Ltd., *Tektronix GPIB Reference Guide.* A useful pocket reference incorporating the comprehensive ASCII/GPIB/IEC code chart

Appendix 1:
Data codes and interfaces

RS 232-C (CCITT V24)

This interface is an earlier design based on a 20 mA current loop circuit and allowing up to ± 25 V levels, a feature not very compatible with modern TTL logic levels. While it is slow in data rate terms due to its serial binary code the current drive does offer reliable long distance transmission and it may be the communication interface of choice for bus extenders. While generally applied to compatible peripherals such as teletypes, printers and magnetic recorders, it is found on a wide range of units and is a frequent control interface on many low-cost computers.

BINARY CODE—WORD-SERIAL, BIT-PARALLEL

The simplest form of transmission; no code conversion is required and high data rates up to 1 M word/s may be run. The memory of many instrument stores are in this format, allowing almost direct connection. Its disadvantage is cable expense since 10 wires per decimal digit are needed (see BCD section following) together with some 20 lines for the interface control; typically 50–80 lines are required. The interface controls and programming are non-standardised and are more or less unique to each installation.

BYTE-SERIAL, BIT-PARALLEL BINARY

Format data words in the word-serial code longer than 8 bits must be broken into two sections to fit on an 8-line data bus.

SERIAL ASCII

Fully alphanumerically coded using an 8-bit word to define each character, the words are transmitted serially and are extensively used in alphanumeric applications such as keyboards, VDUs, etc.

PARALLEL BCD

Using a code, 'Binary Coded Decimal', this simple interface format uses fewer lines than the serial bit-parallel binary by converting each decimal digit to a 4-bit binary equivalent. Its low cost of implementation is offset by its relative inefficiency and lack of standardisation, but it is frequently found on low-cost digital instruments such as DVMs, counters and typically small numeric strip chart recorders which may be directly interconnected.

PARALLEL ASCII

Similar to parallel BCD except that an 8-bit data bus is employed to carry each ASCII character, this relatively fast data format is the central data channel for the IEEE bus.

OTHER INTERFACES

S100: Essentially a computer frame system bus, S100 is commonly used on the interconnect backplane interface for the modular unit cards of a microcomputer.

CAMAC–IEEE-583: A modular block system originating from the nuclear industry for control and monitoring with massive expansion capability, e.g., up to 4,000 interface units on cable runs of 4,000 m. (GPIB 14 units plus controller, 20 m cable excluding extensions.)

HPIL: An inexpensive single loop serial interface developed for advanced pocket calculators to control and communicate with simple instruments.

Appendix 2:
GPIB manufacturers of equipment

CODE FOR INSTRUMENT TYPE LEGENDS

C = Controller (processor, display, storage)
I = Interfaces, connectors, switch boxes
M = Measuring instruments, meters, scopes, contents, etc. (measurements)
P = Peripherals, plotters, etc. (display, storage)
S = Signal sources (stimulus)
T = Test units, specialised measurement
C I M P S T = *All* categories

Adret Electronique
12 Av Vladimir
Komarov
Trappes 78, Yvelines
France
(1) 051 2972
(S, M)

Ailtech Eaton Ltd
Sherwood House
High St
Crowthorne, Berks
RS11 7AT
Great Britain
(03446) 71111
(I, M, S, T)

**Amplicon Electronics
Ltd**
Richmond Rd
Brighton, Sussex
BN2 3RL
Great Britain
(0273) 608331
(I, T)

Apple Computer Inc
10260 Bandley Dr
Cupertino, CA 95014
USA
(408) 996-1010
(C, I)

**Applied Micro
Technology**
Box 3042
Tucson, AZ 85702
USA
(602) 622-8605
(I)

Autek Systems Corp
3200 Coronado Dr
Santa Clara, CA 95051
USA
(408) 496-0400
(T, M)

**Ballantine Laboratories
Inc**
Box 97
Boston, NJ 07005
USA
(201) 335-0900
(M, I, S)

Base^2 Inc
Box 3548
Fullerton, CA 92634
USA
(714) 992-4344
(P)

**Berkeley Nucleonics
Corp**
1198 Tenth St
Berkeley, CA 94710
USA
(415) 527-1121
(S, I)

**Boonton Electronics
Corp**
Box 122
Parsippany, NJ 07054
USA
(201) 887-5110
(M, S)

T G Branden Cop
5565 SE International
Way
Portland, OR 97222
USA
(503) 659-9366
(M)

**Bryans Southern
Instruments Ltd**
Willow Lane
Mitcham, Surrey
CR4 4UL
Great Britain
640-3490
(P)

B & K Ltd
Cross Lances Rd
Hounslow, Middlesex
TW3 2AE
Great Britain
(01) 570-7774
(T, M, S)

Bruel & Kjaer
2850 Naerum
Denmark
02-800500

**Bruel & Kjaer
Instruments Inc**
185 Forest St
Marlboro, MA 01752
USA
(617) 481-7000
(M, S, T)

**California Computer
Systems**
250 Caribbean Dr
Sunnyvale, CA 94086
USA
(408) 734-5811
in UK:
Wego Computers Ltd
22a High St
Caterham, Surrey
CR3 5UA
Great Britain
(0883) 49235

**California Instruments
Div**
Norlin Industries
5150 Convoy St
San Diego, CA 92111
USA
(714) 279-8620
(M)

**Commodore Business
Machines**
Computer Systems Div
950 Rittenhouse Rd
Norristown, PA 19403
USA
(800) 523-5622
(C, I, P)

**Computer Automation
Inc**
Industrial Products Div
2181 DuPont Dr
Irvine, CA 92713
USA
(714) 8333-8830
(C)

**Computer Data Systems
Inc**
186-58 Homestead
Morrison, CO 80465
USA
(303)697-8014
(I)

Comstron/Adret
200 E Sunrise Hwy
Freeport, NY 11520
USA
(516) 546-9700
(S, M)

Control Logic Inc
9 Tech Circle
Natick, MA 01760
USA
(617) 655-1170
(I)

Data General Corp
Rte 9
Westboro, MA 01581
USA
(617) 366-8911
(I, C)

Data Laboratories Ltd
28 Wates Way
Mitcham, Surrey
CF4 4HR
Great Britain
(01) 640-5321
(M)

(See also **Konton
Electronics Inc**)
(C)

Data Precision Div
Analogic Corp
Electronics Av
Danvers, MA 01923
USA
(617) 246-1600
(M, I)

Datatronic AB
Box 42094
S-126 12 Stockholm
Sweden
8-744 59 20
(I)

Datron Electronics Ltd
Meteor Close
Norwich Airport
Industrial Estate
Norwich NR6 6HQ
Great Britain
(0603) 412126
(T, M, C)

Datron Instruments Ltd
Laguna Hills Business
Park
Laguna Hills, CA 92563
USA
(714) 830-8860
(T, M, C)

Digital Equipment Corp
Components Group
1 Iron Way
Marlboro, MA 01752
USA
(617) 467-5111
(I, C)

**Dolch Logic
Instruments GmbH**
Ottostrasse 25
D-6056 Heusenstamm
West Germany
(0 61 04) 64 77-78
(M, T)

**Dolch Logic
Instruments Inc**
230 Devon Dr
San Jose, CA 95112
USA
(408) 998-5730
(M, T)

Dylon Corp
3670 Ruffin Rd
San Diego, CA 92123
USA
(714) 292-5584
(I, P)

**Eagle Signal
Industrial Controls**
Gulf & Western Mfg
Co
736 Federal St
Davenport, IA 52803
USA
(319) 326-8111
(C)

Eaton Corp
Electronic
Instrumentation Div
5340 Alla Rd
Los Angeles, CA 90066
USA
(213) 822-3061
(M, T)

EH International Inc
7303 Edgewater Dr
Oakland, CA 94621
USA
(415) 638-5656
(M, S)

EIP Microwave Inc
2731 N First St
San Jose, CA 95134
USA
(408) 946-5700
(M)

Electro-Metrics Div
Penril Corp
100 Church St
Amsterdam, NY 12010
USA
(518) 843-2600
(I)

**Electronic Development
Corp**
11 Hamlin St
Boston, MA 02127
USA
(617) 268-9696
(M)

**Electro Scientific
Industries Ltd**
13900 NW Science
Park Dr
Portland, OR 97229
USA
(503) 641-4141
(M, S)

Elgar Corp
Onan Power Systems
Co
8225 Mercury Ct
San Diego, CA 92111
USA
(714) 565-1155
(S)

Epson America Inc
3415 Kashiwa St
Torrance, CA 90506
USA
(213) 539-9140
(P)

Exact Electronics Inc
Box 347
Tillamook, OR 97141
USA
(503) 842-8441
(S)

Fairchild Semiconductor
464 Ellis St
Mt View, CA 94042
USA
(415) 962-5011
(T)

Farnell Instruments Ltd
Sand Beck Way
Wetherby
West Yorkshire
LS22 4DH
Great Britain
(0937) 61961

John Fluke Mfg Co Inc
Box C9090
Everett, WA 98206
USA
(206) 342-6300
(All)

GenRad Inc
300 Baker Ave
Concord, MA 01742
USA
(617) 369-4400
(M, T)

**Gould Inc Instruments
Div**
3631 Perkins Ave
Cleveland, OH 44114
USA
(216) 361-3315
(T, M, S)

**Gould Inc Instruments
Div**
4600 Old Ironsides Dr
Santa Clara, CA 95050
USA
(408) 988-6800
(T, M, S)

**Gould Inc Instruments
Div**
Roebuck Rd
Hainault, Essex
Great Britain
(01) 500-1000

**Grumman Aerospace
Corp**
Integrated Logistics
Support Dept
ATE Systems—Plant 31
Bethpage, NY 11714
USA
(516) 575-7007
(S, M, T)

**Guildline Instruments
Inc**
2 Westchester Plaza
Elmsford, NY 10523
USA
(914) 592-9101
(I, M)

Gulton Industries Inc
Measurement &
Control Systems Div
Gulton Industrial Park
East Greenwich, RI
02818
USA
(401) 884-6800
(P)

Hewlett-Packard Co
1507 Page Mill Rd
Palo Alto, CA 94304
USA
Phone local office
(All)

ICS Electronics Corp
1620 Zanker Rd
San Jose, CA 95112
USA
(408) 298-4844
(T, C, I)

**Information
Development
& Applications Inc**
10759 Tucker St
Beltsville, MD 20705
USA
(301) 937-3600
(P)

**Innovative Data
Technology**
4060 Morena Blvd
San Diego, CA 92117
USA
(714) 270-3990
(P)

Intech Instruments Div
282 Brokaw Rd
Santa Clara, CA 95050
USA
(408) 727-0500
(I)

Intel Corp
3065 Bowers Ave
Santa Clara, CA 95051
USA
(408) 987-8080
(I)

Intel Corp
OEM Microcomputer
Systems Operation
5200 NE Elam Young
Parkway
Hillsboro, OR 97123
USA
(503) 640-7147
(I)

Interface Technology
150 E Arrow Hwy
San Dimas, CA 91773
USA
(714) 599-0840
(C, I)

Intersil
10710 N Tantau Ave
Cupertino, CA 95014
USA
(408) 996-5000
(I)

**Interstate Electronics
Corp**
Subsidiary of A-T-O
Corp
1001 E Ball Rd
Box 3117
Anaheim, CA 92803
USA
(S)

Ithaco Inc
735 W Clinton St
Ithaca, NY 14850
USA
(607) 272-7640
(M)

Keithley Instruments Inc
28775 Aurora Rd
Cleveland, OH 44139
USA
(216) 248-0400
(M, S, T)

Kepco Inc
131-38 Sanford Ave
Flushing, NY 11352
USA
(212) 461-7000
(S)

Kemo Ltd
12 Goodwood Parade
Elmers End
Beckenham, Kent
BR3 3QZ
Great Britain
(01) 558-3838
(T)

**Kikusui International
Corp**
17819 S Figueroa St
Gardena, CA 90248
USA
(213) 515-6432
(I, M, S)

Kinetic Systems Corp
11 Maryknoll Dr
Lockport, IL 60441
USA
(815) 838-0005
(I)

Kontron Electronics Inc
630 Price Ave
Redwood City, CA
94063
USA
(415) 361-1012
(C, M)

**Kontron Elektronik
GmbH**
Breshuer Strasse 2
8057 Eching
West Germany
(089) 31901-1
(C, M)

Krohn-Hite Corp
Avon Industrial Park
Avon, MA 02322
USA
(617) 580-1660
(M, S, T)

**Lambda Electronics
Corp**
Veeco Instruments Inc
515 Broad Hollow Rd
Melville, NY 11747
USA
(516) 694-4200
(S)

**Leader Instruments
Corp**
380 Oser Ave
Hauppauge, NY 11787
USA
(516) 231-6900
(M)

LeCroy California
1806 Embarcadero Rd
Palo Alto, CA 94303
USA
(415) 856-1800
(I, T)

Marconi Electronics Inc
100 Stonehurst Ct
Northvale, NJ 07647
USA
(201) 767-7250
(M, S, T)

**Marconi Instruments
Ltd**
Longacres
St Albans, Herts
Great Britain
(0) 727-59292
(M, S, T)

Matrix Corp
1717 S Saunders St
Raleigh, NC 27603
USA
(919) 833-2837
(I)

MDB Systems Inc
1995 N Batavia St
Orange, CA 92665
USA
(714) 998-6900
(I)

**Microcomputer Systems
Corp**
432 Lakeside Dr
Sunnyvale, CA 94086
USA
(408) 733-4200
(P)

Micro-Tel Corp
6310 Blair Hill Lane
Baltimore, MD 21209
USA
(303) 823-6227
(S)

Motorola Inc
Bipolar Integrated
Circuits Group
Box 20912
Phoenix, AZ 85036
USA
(I)

Motorola Inc
Microsystems
Operation
3102 N 56th St
Phoenix, AZ 85018
USA
(602) 244-5714
(I)

Motorola Inc
MOS Integrated Circuit
Group
3501 Ed Bluestein Blvd
Austin, TX 78712
USA
(512) 928-6800
(I)

National Instruments
8900 Shoal Creek Rd
Austin, TX 78758
USA
(512) 454-3526
(I)

**National (Japan)
Matsushita**
National Panasonic
Whitby Rd
Slough, Bucks
Great Britain
(M, S, T)

Neff Instrument Corp
1088 E Hamilton Rd
Duarte, CA 91010
USA
(213) 357-2281
(I)

Nicolet Instrument Corp
Oscilloscope Div
5225 Verona Rd
Madison, WI 53711
USA
(608) 271-3333
(M, T)

**Nicolet Paratronics
Corp**
2140 Bering Dr
San Jose, CA 95131
USA
(408) 263-2252
(C, M)

Nicolet Scientific Corp
80a Emscote Rd
Warwick
Great Britain
(0926) 44111
(M)

Nicolet Scientific Corp
245 Livingston St
Northvale, NJ 07647
USA
(201) 767-7100

Norland Corp
Norland Dr
Ft Atkinson, WI 53538
USA
(414) 563-8456
(T)

**North Atlantic
Industries**
60 Plane Ave
Hauppauge, NY 11787
USA
(516) 582-6500
(M)

Ortofon Feldon Audio
126 Great Portland St
London W1N 5PH
Great Britain
(01) 580-4314
(T, M)

**Pacific Measurements
Inc**
488 Tasman Dr
Sunnyvale, CA 94086
USA
(408) 734-5780
(M)

Pedersen Instruments
2772 Camino Diablo
Walnut Creek, CA
94596
USA
(415) 937-3630
(P)

**NV Philips
Gloeilampenfabrieken**
Test & Measuring Dept
TQ 111-2
Eindhoven
Netherlands
(All)

**Philips Test &
Measuring Instruments
Inc**
85 McKee Dr
Mahwah, NJ 07430
USA
(201) 529-3800
(All)

Physical Data Inc
8089 SW Cirrus Dr
Beaverton, OR 97005
USA
(503) 644-9014
(C, M)

Pickles & Trout
Box 1206
Goleta, CA 93116
USA
(805) 685-4641
(I)

Polarad Electronics Inc
5 Delaware Dr
Lake Success, NY
11042
USA
(516) 328-1100
(M)

PPM Ltd
Hermitage Rd
St Johns
Woking, Surrey
GU21 1TZ
Great Britain
(04867) 80111 (I, M)

Precision Filters Inc
303 W Lincoln St
Ithaca, NY 14850
USA
(607) 277-3550
(M)

**Programmed Test
Sources Inc**
Beaverbrook Rd
Littleton, MA 01460
USA
(617) 486-3008 (S)

**Prosser Scientific
Instruments Ltd**
Lady Lane Industrial
Estate
Hadleigh
Ipswich, Suffolk
IP7 6DQ
Great Britain
(0473) 823005
(M, S, T)

**Racal-Dana Instruments
Inc**
18912 Von Karman Ave
Box C-19541
Irvine, CA 92713
USA
(714) 833-1234
(All)

Racal Instruments
Duke St
Windsor, Berks
SL4 1SB
Great Britain
(All)

**Radiometer Electronics
US Inc**
31029 Center Ridge Rd
Westlake, OH 44145
USA
(216) 871-7617
(I, M, S, T)

**Radiometer Electronics
Inc**
Danbridge Ltd
Sherwood House
High St
Crawthorne, Berks
Great Britain
(I, M, S, T)

Rair Microcomputer Corp
4101 Burton Dr
Santa Clara, CA 95050
USA
(408) 988-1790
(C)

RBI Systems
Box 6393
Silver Spring, MD 20906
USA
(301) 949-0430
(T)

Real Time Systems Inc
152 S MacQuesten Parkway
Mt Vernon, NY 10550
USA
(914) 667-0425
(S)

Rockwell International
Electronic Devices Div
3310 Miraloma Ave
Box 3669
Anaheim, CA 92803
USA
(C, I)

Rohde & Schwarz GmbH & Co
Muehldorfstr 15
D-8000 Munich
West Germany
(089) 4129-1
(C, I, M, S, T)

Rohde & Schwarz Sales Co
14 Gloria Lane
Fairfield, NJ 07006
USA
(201) 575-0750
(C, I, M, S, T)

Rotek Instrument Corp
220 Grove St
Waltham, MA 02154
USA
(617) 899-4611
(M)

Signetics Corp
Box 409
Sunnyvale, CA 94086
USA
(400) 746-1675
(I)

Solartron Ltd
Farnborough, Hampshire
Great Britain
(0252) 44433
(I, M, S, T)

Soltec Corp
11684 Pendleton St
Sun Valley, CA 91352
USA
(213) 767-0044
(P)

Spectral Dynamics
Box 671
San Diego, CA 92112
USA
(714) 268-7100
(M, S, T)

Scientific Engineering Laboratories
11 Neil Dr
Old Bethpage, NY 11804
USA
(516) 694-3205
(I)

SSM Microcomputer Products
2190 Paragon Dr
San Jose, CA 95131
USA
(408) 946-7400
(I)

Star Micronics Inc
200 Park Ave
New York, NY 10166
USA
(212) 986-6700
(P)

Summagraphics Corp
35 Brentwood Ave
Fairfield, CT 06430
USA
(203) 384-1344
(P)

Systel Computers Inc
538 Oakmead Parkway
Sunnyvale, CA 94086
USA
(C)

Systron-Donner Instrument Div
2727 Systron Dr
Concord, CA 94518
USA
(415) 676-5000
(C, I, M, S, T)

Systron-Donner Instrument Div
St Mary's Rd
Leamington Spa
Warwickshire CV31 1Q
Great Britain
(0926) 3541
(All)

Takeda Riken Industry Co Ltd
UK Distr MIT Ltd
Greenhill Industrial Estate
Riddings, Derbys DE55 4DA
Great Britain
(0773) 604411
(S, M)

Tektronix Inc
Box 4828
Portland, OR 97208
USA
(800) 547-6711
(800) 452-6773 (in OR)
(All)

Tektronix (UK) Ltd
Coldharbour Lane
Harpenden, Herts
AL5 4UP
Great Britain
(05827) 63141
(All)

Texas Instruments Inc
Box 1443, M/S 6404
Houston, TX 77001
USA
(713) 776-6511
(T)

**Three Rivers Computer
Corp**
160 N Craig St
Pittsburgh, PA 15213
USA
(412) 621-6250
(C)

Tri-Data
505 E Middlefield Rd
Mt View, CA 94043
USA
(415) 969-3700
(P)

Valhalla Scientific Inc
7576 Trade St
San Diego, CA 92121
USA
(714) 578-8280
(M)

Victor Data Products
3900 N Rockwell Ave
Chicago, IL 60618
USA
(312) 539-8200
(P)

WangmLaboratories Inc
1 Industrial Ave
Lowell, MA 01851
USA
(617) 851-4111
(T)

**Wandel u Goltermann
GmbH**
Box 45
D-7412 Eningen u A
West Germany
(0) 721891-1
(M, T)

W&G Instruments Inc
119Naylon Ave
Livingston, NJ 07039
USA
(201) 994-0854
(M)

**Watanabe Instruments
Corp**
UK Environmental
Equipments Northern
Ltd
64 Welsh Row
Nantwich, Cheshire
CW5 5ES
Great Britain
(0270) 65115
(P)

Wavetek
9045 Balboa Ave
San Diego, CA 92123
USA
(714) 279-2200
(I, S, M)

Wavetek Rockland Inc
Rockleigh Industrial
Park
Rockleigh, NJ 07647
USA
(201) 767-7900
(S, M)

Weinschel Engineering
1 Weinschel Lane
Gaithersburg, MD
20760
USA
(301) 948-3434
(S)

Wiltron Co
805 E Middlefield Rd
Mt View, CA 94043
USA
(415) 969-6500
(T, M, S)

Wyle Labs
3200 Magruder Blvd
Hampton, VA 23666
USA
(804) 838-0122
(C)

Ziatech
2410 Broad St
San Luis Obispo,
CA 93401
USA
(805) 541-0488
(I, T)

Appendix 3: Recommended units and symbols

Basic SI units	Common usage	Representation
metre	m	M
kilogram	kg	KG
second	s	S
ampere	A	A
kelvin	K	K
mole	mol	MOL
candela	cd	CD

Other units	Common usage	Representation
grade (angle)	g (s)	CON
degree (angle)	° (s)	DEG
minute (angle)	′ (s)	MNT
second (angle)	″ (s)	SEC
litre	l	L
minute (time)	min	MIN
hour	h	HR
day	d	D
year	a	ANN
gram	g	G
tonne	t	TNE
bar	bar	BAR
poise	P	P
stokes	St	ST
electronvolt	eV	EV
degree celsius	°C	CEL
atomic mass unit	u	U

Derived SI units	Common usage	Representation
hertz	Hz	HZ
newton	N	N
pascal	Pa	PA
joule	J	J
watt	W	W
coulomb	C	C
volt	V	V
farad	F	F
ohm	Ω	OHM
siemens	S	SIE
weber	Wb	WB
tesla	T	T
henry	H	H
lumen	lm	LM
lux	lx	LX
bel	B	B

Multipliers	Factor by which the unit is multiplied	International symbol (common use symbol)	Representation
tera	10^{12}	T	T
giga	10^{9}	G	G
mega	10^{6}	M	MA
kilo	10^{3}	k	K
hecto	10^{2}	h	H
deca	10	da	DA
deci	10^{-1}	d	D
centi	10^{-2}	c	C
milli	10^{-3}	m	M
micro	10^{-6}	μ	U
nano	10^{-9}	n	N
pico	10^{-12}	p	P
femto	10^{-15}	f	F
atto	10^{-18}	a	A

Appendix 4:
IEC-625: IEEE-488 mnemonics and their definitions

Capitalised mnemonics represent interface states and remote messages, while lower case mnemonics indicate local messages received via interface functions.

AC	Addressed command
ACDS	Accept data state
ACG	Addressed command group
ACRS	Acceptor ready state
AD	Addressed
AH	Acceptor handshake
AH1	Complete capability
AH10	No capability
AIDS	Acceptor idle state
ANRS	Acceptor not ready state
ANSI	American National Standards Institute
APRS	Affirmative poll response state
ATN	Attention
AWNS	Acceptor wait for new cycle state
C	Controller
CACS	Controller addressed state
CADS	Controller idle state
CAWS	Controller active wait state
CIDS	Controller idle state
CPPS	Controller parallel poll state
CPWS	Controller parallel poll wait state
CSBS	Controller standby state
CSNS	Controller service not requested state
CSRS	Controller service requested state
CSWS	Controller synchronous wait state
CTRS	Controller transfer state
DAB	Data byte
DAC	Data accepted

DAV	Data valid
DC	Device clear
DCAS	Device clear active states
DCIS	Device clear idle state
DCL	Device clear
DD	Device dependent
DIO	Data input
DT	Device trigger
DTAS	Device trigger active state
DTIS	Device trigger state
END	End
EOI	End or identify
EOS	End of string
F	Active false
(F)	Passive false
GET	Group execute trigger
GTL	Go to local
gts	Go to standby
IDY	Identify
IFC	Interface clear
ist	Individual status
L or LE	Listener or extended listener
LACS	Listener active state
LADS	Listener addressed state
LAG	Listen address group
LIDS	Listener idle state
LLO	Local lockout
LOCS	Local state
lon	Listen only
LPAS	Listener primary addressed state
[lpe]	Local poll enable
LPIS	Listener primary idle state
ltn	Listen
lun	Local unlisten
LWLS	Local with lockout state
M	Multiline
MLA or [MLA]	My listen address
MSA or [MSA]	My secondary address
MTA or [MTA]	My talk address
nba	New byte available

NDAC	Not data accepted
NPRS	Negative poll response state
NRFD	Not ready for data
NUL	Null byte
OSA	Other secondary address
OTA	Other talk address
PACS	Parallel poll addressed to configure state
PCG	Primary command group
POFS	Power off
pon	Power on
PP	Parallel poll
PPAS	Parallel poll active state
PPC	Parallel poll configure
PPD or [PPD]	Parallel poll disable
PPE or [PPE]	Parallel poll enable
PPIS	Parallel poll idle state
PPR	Parallel poll response
PPSS	Parallel poll standby state
PPU	Parallel poll unconfigure
PUCS	Parallel poll unaddressed to configure state
rdy	Ready (for next message)
REMS	Remote state
REN	Remote enable
RFD	Ready for data
RL	Remote local
rpp	Request parallel poll
RQS	Request service
rsc	Request system control
rsv	Request service
rtl	Return to local
RWLS	Remote with lockout state
SACS	System control active state
SCG	Secondary command group
SDC or [[SDC]	Selected device clear
SDYS	Source delay state
SE	Secondary
SGNS	Source generate state
SH	Source handshake
SIAS	System central interface clear active state
sic	Send interface clear
SIDS	Source idle state
SIIS	System control interface clear idle state

SINS	System control interface clear not active state
SIWS	Source idle wait state
SNAS	System control not active state
SPAS	Serial poll active state
SPD	Serial poll disable
SPE	Serial poll enable
SPIS	Serial poll idle state
SPMS	Serial poll mode state
SR	Service request
SRAS	System control remote enable active state
sre	Send remote enable
SRIS	System control remote enable idle state
SRNS	System control remote enable not active state
SRQ	Service request
SRQS	Service request state
ST	Status
STB	Status byte
STRS	Source transfer state
SWNS	Source wait for new cycle state
T or (TE)	Talker or extended talker
T	Active true
(T)	Passive true
TACS	Talker active state
TADS	Talker addressed state
TAG	Talk address group
tca	Take control asynchronously
tcs	Take control synchronously
TCT or [TCT]	Take control
TIDS	Talker idle state
ton	Talk only
TPAS	Talker primary addressed state
TPIS	Talker primary idle state
U	Uniline message
UC	Universal command
UCG	Universal command group
UNL	Unlisten
UNT	Untalk

Appendix 5:
Glossary of terms

ACCEPTOR: A device receiving multiline remote messages from the GPIB in either the command or the data mode.

ACG: Addressed Command Group.

ACTIVE CONTROLLER: There may be more than one controller in a system, but only one can be active at a time.

ADDRESS: A 7-bit code applied to the GPIB by the active controller to select instruments as talker or listener Addresses are multiline interface messages.

ADDRESS SWITCHES: Switches on the front or rear panel of a device, used to assign an address to that device.

ADDRESSED BUS COMMANDS: Commands allowing the active controller to influence only those devices which have been addressed. They can be used to initiate simultaneous actions.

ATN: Attention line. The ATN signal is generated by the active controller to indicate the transfer mode to be used. In the command mode ATN = 'true' and in the data mode ATN = 'false'.

BIDIRECTIONAL BUS: A bus which any individual device can use for two-way (input and output) transmission of messages.

BIT: The smallest part of a character (byte) containing intelligible information.

BLOCK: See Message unit

BUS: A signal line or lines used by an interface system over which messages are carried and to which several devices may be connected.

BUS COMMANDS: A group of special codes from the primary command group which are sent over the bus by the active controller to devices, to initiate certain types of operation within those devices capable of responding these codes.

Each instrument on the GPIB is designed to respond to those codes that have a useful meaning for it, and to ignore all others.

Bus commands can be subdivided into unaddress bus commands, universal bus commands and addressed bus commands.

BUS HANDSHAKE: A three-line handshake between the interface sections of devices via the GPIB.

BUS LINE: One of the 16 lines of the GPIB.

BYTE: A character sent over the data bus, normally consisting of seven bits.

COMMAND MODE: In this mode (ATN = 'true') the bus is used by the controller to send multiline interface messages like addresses and bus commands.

COMPATIBILITY: The degree to which devices may be interconnected and operated without modification.

CONTROLLER: Any device on the GPIB which is capable of setting the ATN line to determine the transmission mode, sending bus commands and addressing devices on the bus as talkers and/or listeners.

CONTROL MESSAGE: Same as interface Message.

DAB: Data Byte.

DATA BUS: The 8 lines (DIO 1–8) of the GPIB used to transfer (multiline) remote messages.

DATA BYTES: These multiline device-dependent messages can be sent by an addressed talker as measurement data or received by an addressed listener as display data.

DATA BYTE TRANSFER CONTROL LINES: See Handshake Lines.

DATA FIELD: Part of a message unit to identify portions of data within the message unit.

DATA MODE: In this mode (ATN = 'false') the bus is used to transmit device-dependent messages, i.e. data bytes, programming instructions, display data, measurement data or status bytes, from a source to an acceptor.

DAV: Handshake bus line 'Data Valid'.

DCL: Universal bus command Device Clear.

DELIMITER: Part of a device-dependent message used to separate the elements of the message. There is a string delimiter, a block delimiter and a record delimiter.

DEVICE: Instrument on the bus with GPIB interface facilities. A device can be subdivided into a 'GPIB Interface' section and a 'device functions' section.

DEVICE-DEPENDENT MESSAGE: These messages are generally transferred between an addressed talker and one or more addressed listeners in the data mode. They can be sub-divided into measurement data, display data, status bytes and programming instructions.

DEVICE FUNCTIONS: The part of a device that can be developed independently of the requirements of the bus, and embodying the basic functions of the instrument.

DEVICE HANDSHAKE: A two-line handshake between the device functions and the GPIB interface part of a device.

DIO: The 'Data Input/Output' lines of the bus, namely the data bus.

DISPLAY DATA: A device-dependent message indicating text or other data to be displayed on or stored in a device.

END: End (of a data string).

EOI: General interface-management bus line 'End or Identify'.

EOS: End of String—Delimiter.

ESCAPE SEQUENCE: A data shift technique which can be used to select programming instructions and display data in cases where a device can receive both types of device-dependent messages.

EXTENDED LISTENER: An instrument with two address bytes in its listen address.

EXTENDED TALKER: A device with two address bytes in its talk address.

EXTENDED ADDRESS: An address composed of two 7-bit codes, the primary address and secondary address, used to select an extended listener or an extended talker.

GENERAL INTERFACE MANAGEMENT LINES: A group of 5 lines (ATN, IFC, REN, SRQ and EOI) in the bus; each line has a specific function for communication between the controller and other devices.

GET: Addressed bus command 'Group Execute Trigger'.

GPIB: The IEEE-488, IEC-625 standards and recommendations for connecting instruments in a bus system. (GPIB—general purpose interface bus, often referred to as 'bus'.)

GTL: Addressed bus command 'Go To Local'.

HANDSHAKE LINES: The DAV, NRFD and NDAC lines of the bus. These lines control the transfer of multiline messages from a source to an acceptor over the data bus.

HANDSHAKE PROCEDURE: The sequence of events on the bus during transfer of a multiline remote message between a source and one or more acceptors. The three handshake lines control this procedure.

IDY: Interface message 'Identify'.

IEC: International Electrotechnical Commission.

IEEE: US Electronic standards body for the 488 and 728 documents covering the GPIB.

IFC: General interface-management bus line 'Interface Clear'.

INTERFACE: A shared boundary between the system in question and another system, or between parts of a system, through which information is conveyed.

INTERFACE BUS: See GPIB.

INTERFACE FUNCTIONS: System elements of the GPIB interface which provide the basic operational facilities through which a device can receive, process and send messages. A number of interface functions, each of which acts in accordance with a special protocol, are defined in the recommendations.

INTERFACE FUNCTION SUBSET: An interface function can have one or more allowable subsets with different capabilities.

INTERFACE MESSAGE: A message which can cause a state transition in the interface functions of the GPIB interface section of a device. Addresses and bus commands are examples of multiline interface messages.

Typical uniline interface messages are ATN and IFC.

Multiline interface messages are sent in the command mode.

INTERFACE SYSTEM: A group of bus-compatible instruments interconnected via the GPIB.

LAG: Listen Address Group.

LISTEN ADDRESS: An address which selects one device as data receiver (listener) but does not affect the other listeners.

LISTENER: A device that is able to receive device-dependent data from the bus after it is addressed with its listen address by the controller in charge.

LLO: Universal bus command 'Local Lockout'.

LOCAL CONTROL: A method whereby a device is programmable by means of its front-panel controls in order to enable the device to perform different tasks (also referred to as 'manual control').

LOCAL MESSAGE: Any message between the device functions and the interface of a device.

MEASURING DATA: A device-dependent message indicating the measurement results of an instrument.

MESSAGE: Coded information transferred digitally via signal lines.

MESSAGE UNIT: The smallest possible unit of information of a device-dependent message. A message unit is partitioned into data fields. In general, a message unit contains a header, a body and a delimiter. A string (=message unit) is a sequence of characters constituting a related data set. A block is a sequence of related data strings and a record is a sequence of related data blocks.

MLA: My Listen Address.

MSA: My Secondary Address.

MTA: My Talk Address.

MULTILINE MESSAGE: A remote message which shares a group of bus lines, the data bus.

   Only one multiline message can be sent at a time.

NDAC: Handshake bus line 'Not Data Accepted'.

NRFD: Handshake bus line 'Not Ready For Data'.

NUL: Null byte (all eight bits are false).

OSA: Other Secondary Address.

OTA: Other Talk Address.

OUTPUT MESSAGE: A message originating in an interface function of the bus interface of a device. It may be a remote message or a local message.

PARALLEL POLLING: A method of simultaneously checking status (e.g. request for service) on up to eight devices on the bus at the same time. Each device is assigned to a DIO line to indicate whether it requests service or not.

PCG: Primary Command Group.

PPC: Addressed bus command 'Parallel Poll Configure'.

PPD: Secondary command 'Parallel Poll Disable'.

PPE: Secondary command 'Parallel Poll Enable'.

PPR: Parallel Poll Response.

PPU: Universal bus command 'Parallel Poll Unconfigure'.

PRIMARY ADDRESS: The first part of an extended address, which may be a normal talk address or listen address.

PRIMARY COMMAND: An interface message giving one of the codes of the primary command group, e.g. an address or a bus command.

PROGRAM COMMAND: A programming instruction used to send a single byte (e.g. start or reset) for remote control of an instrument with commands.

PROGRAM DATA: A programming instruction used to send multi-byte data (e.g. range or frequency of an instrument) to remote-control functions.

PROGRAMMABLE INSTRUMENT: An instrument (device) which performs specified operations (including transmission of the results of its measurements to the system, if it is a measuring instrument) on command from the system.

RECORD: See Message Unit.

REMOTE CONTROL: A method whereby a device is programmable via its electrical interface connection by programming instructions over the bus in order to enable the device to perform different tasks.

REMOTE MESSAGE: Any message, uniline or multiline, transferred over the bus.

Remote messages can be subdivided into interface messages and device-dependent messages.

REN: General interface-management bus line 'Remote Enable'.

RQS: Requested Service.

SCG: Secondary Command Group.

SDC: Addressed bus command 'Selective Device Clear'.

SECONDARY COMMAND: An interface message giving one of the codes of the secondary command group, which is only operative after a primary command has been given, e.g. a secondary address or a PPE command after a PPC command.

SERIAL POLLING: A method of sequentially determining which device connected to the bus has requested service. Only one instrument is checked at a time, while its status byte is read by the controller.

SIGNAL: The physical representation of information.

SOURCE: A device transmitting multiline remote messages on the GPIB in either the command or the data mode.

SPD: Universal bus command 'Serial Poll Disable'.

SPE: Universal bus command 'Serial Poll Enable'.

SRQ: General interface-management bus line 'Service Request'.

STATUS BYTE: Device-dependent message with coded information about the status of the device functions. In the Serial Poll mode such a status byte can be sent by the device in the data mode after the latter has been addressed as talker.

STATUS DATA: A device-dependent message indicating the actual status of a device. It incorporates the RQS message and the STB message. See Status Byte.

STB: Status byte.

STRING: See Message Unit.

SYSTEM: Set of interconnected elements constituted to achieve a given objective by performing a specified function.

SYSTEM CONTROLLER: A device on the IEC bus which has all

the features of a standard controller plus the ability to control the IFC and REN lines.

TAG: Talk Address Group.

TALKER: A device that is able to transmit data on the GPIB after it is addressed with its talk address by the active controller.

TALK ADDRESS: An address which selects one device as data source (talker) and disables all other potential talkers.

TCT: Addressed bus command 'Take Control'.

UCG: Universal Command Group.

UNADDRESS BUS COMMAND: Bus command obeyed by all addressable devices. The unlisten bus command unaddresses all listeners, while the untalk bus command unaddresses the active talker.

UNILINE MESSAGE: A remote message sent over a single bus line.

UNIVERSAL BUS COMMAND: Bus command affecting every device on the bus capable of responding, regardless of whether they have been addressed or not. Examples are Device Clear (DCL) and Serial Poll Enable (SPE).

UNIVERSAL COMMAND: Command causing every instrument on the bus equipped to do so to perform a specific interface operation, e.g. a (multiline) universal bus command and the uniline messages Interface Clear (IFC), Attention (ATN) and Remote Enable (REN).

UNL: Bus Command 'Unlisten'.

UNT: Bus command 'Untalk'.

Appendix 6:
Descriptions of interface function capabilities

It is recommended that data sheets indicate, in symbolic form (as a minimum), the set of interface functions provided by the subject device. Additional short descriptive phrases, as shown below, are useful where space permits. Specific interface functions may not be included in a product, in which case 'no capability' may be expressed by 0 (e.g., C0).

Source Handshake Function (SH)
  SH1   Complete capability.

Acceptor Handshake Function (AH)
  AH1   Complete capability.

Talker Function (T)
  T1   Basic Talker, Serial Poll, Talk Only Mode.
  T2   Basic Talker, Serial Poll.
  T3   Basic Talker, Talk Only Mode.
  T4   Basic Talker.
  T5   Basic Talker, Serial Poll, Talk Only Mode, Unaddress if MLA.
  T6   Basic Talker, Serial Poll, Unaddress if MLA.
  T7   Basic Talker, Talk Only Mode, Unaddress if MLA.
  T8   Basic Talker, Unaddress if MLA.

Extended Talker Function (TE)
  TE1   Basic Talker, Serial Poll, Talk Only Mode.
  TE2   Basic Talker, Serial Poll.
  TE3   Basic Talker, Talk Only Mode.
  TE4   Basic Talker.
  TE5   Basic Talker, Serial Poll, Talk Only Mode, Unaddress if MSA^LPAS.
  TE6   Basic Talker, Serial Poll, Unaddress if MSA^LPAS.
  TE7   Basic Talker, Talk Only Mode, Unaddress if MSA^LPAS.

Listener Function (L)
- L1   Basic Listener, Listen Only Mode.
- L2   Basic Listener.
- L3   Basic Listener, Listen Only Mode, Unaddress if MTA.
- L4   Basic Listener, Unaddress if MTA.

Extended Listener Function (LE)
- LE1   Basic Listener, Listen Only Mode.
- LE2   Basic Listener.
- LE3   Basic Listener, Listen Only Mode, Unaddress if MSA^TPAS.
- LE4   Basic Listener, Unaddress if MSA^TPAS.

Service Request Function (SR)
- SR1   Complete capability.

Remote Local Function (RL)
- RL1   Complete capability.
- RL2   Without local lock out.

Parallel Poll Function (PP)
- PP1   Remote Configuration.
- PP2   Local Configuration only.

Device Clear Function (DC)
- DC1   Complete capability.
- DC2   Without selective device clear.

Device Trigger Function (DT)
- DT1   Complete capability.

Controller Function (C)

SYMBOL SHORT DESCRIPTION
- C1   System Controller.
- C2   Send IFC and Take Charge.
- C3   Send REN.
- C4   Respond to SRQ.

Note: Only one of the following applies to a given product
- C5   Send Interface Messages, Receive Control, Pass Control, Pass Control to Self, Parallel Poll, Take Control Synchronously.
- C6   Send Interface Messages, Receive Control, Pass Control, Pass Control to Self, Parallel Poll.
- C7   Send Interface Messages, Receive Control, Pass Control, Pass Control to Self, Take Control Synchronously.
- C8   Send Interface Messages, Receive Control, Pass Control, Pass Control to Self.

C9   Send Interface Messages, Receive Control, Pass Control, Parallel Poll, Take Control Synchronously.

C10   Send Interface Messages, Receive Control, Pass Control, Parallel Poll.

C11   Send Interface Messages, Receive Control, Pass Control, Take Control Synchronously.

C12   Send Interface Messages, Receive Control, Pass Control.

C13   Send Interface Messages, Receive Control, Parallel Poll, Take Control Synchronously.

C14   Send Interface Messages, Receive Control, Parallel Poll.

C15   Send Interface Messages, Receive Control, Take Control Synchronously.

C16   Send Interface Messages, Receive Control.

C17   Send Interface Messages, Pass Control, Pass Control to Self, Parallel Poll, Take Control Synchronously.

C18   Send Interface Messages, Pass Control, Pass Control to Self, Parallel Poll.

C19   Send Interface Messages, Pass Control, Pass Control to Self, Take Control Synchronously.

C20   Send Interface Messages, Pass Control, Pass Control to Self.

C21   Send Interface Messages, Pass Control, Parallel Poll, Take Control Synchronously.

C22   Send Interface Messages, Pass Control, Parallel Poll.

C23   Send Interface Messages, Pass Control, Take Control Synchronously.

C24   Send Interface Messages, Pass Control.

C25   Send Interface Messages, Parallel Poll, Take Control Synchronously.

C26   Send Interface Messages, Parallel Poll.

C27   Send Interface Messages, Take Control Synchronously.

C28   Send Interface Messages.

Description of Time Values

Data Rates for DAB Messages
 (1) Characteristic data input rate (when addressed to listen).
      For example: N kilobytes per second.
 (2) Characteristic data output rate (when addressed to talk).
      For example: N kilobytes per second.

Other Time Values
    For example: interface handshake time out.

Description of Device-Dependent Messages
    Most descriptive information will, in fact, be device dependent and

therefore specific examples are not given. The following lists serve as reminders for the types of information thought to be useful for inclusion on data sheets.

Messages to Device Functions
  (1) Identification of programmable controls (remote accessible).
       For example: level, frequency, range.
  (2) Code set(s) used and purpose for each.
       For example: ISO 646 code set for program data: binary for digitizer data.
  (3) Format of program data messages.
       For example: NR1 representation for program data.
  (4) Nominal response time to device commands.
       For example: counter reset time in milliseconds.
  (5) Code assignments and response to unassigned codes.
       For example: M = mode, F = frequency, T = trigger.

Messages from Device Functions
  (1) Identification of output data types.
       For example: NR3 representation for measurement data.
  (2) Code set(s) used and purpose for each.
       For example: ISO 646 for measurement data.
  (3) Format of measurement data messages.
       For example: 4 character header followed by NR3 value.
  (4) Separator codes and purpose(s).
       For example: |,| between amplitude and phase; |NL| between reading sets; END terminates measurement sequence.
  (5) Bit assignment for status data (STB) messages.
       For example: RQS = bit 7; current limit = bit 1; program error = bit 6; coding 1 = true (e.g., coding and descriptive phrases for use).
  (6) Parallel poll bit assignment(s).
       For example: ready = bit 1; limit condition = bit 7.

Address Capabilities*
  (1) Code set available for listen addresses.
       For example: codes 2/0 through 3/14.
  (2) Code set available for talk addresses.
       For example: codes 4/0 through 4/15 only.
  (3) Factory set addresses.
       For example: MLA = 2/7, MTA = 4/7.
  (4) Special address features.
       For example: address 2/7 = raw data; address 2/8 = processed data.
* The column/row location is ISO/ASCII code; letter N = 4/14.

Electrical Driver/Receiver Capabilities

Signal lines with open collector drivers $=E1$

Signal lines with three-state drivers $=E2$

Receiver Type
  For example: Schmitt trigger hysteresis.

Marking

IEC 625 Symbol

Index